Caffeinated
Learning

How to *Design*
and *Conduct Rich, Robust*
Professional Training

Anne M. Beninghof

www.IdeasForEducators.com

ISBN-13: 978-0-692-22535-6

Table of Contents

Chapter

Introduction

It was time to pull my first all-nighter. During my first semester of college, my roommate and I had both been assigned to Mr. Seager's 8:00 a.m. chemistry class. Mr. Seager was a science whiz. Tall and thin, with a scruffy face and rumpled clothing, he fit the stereotype of a scientist. Chemistry was his first love, as evidenced by the number of coffee mugs on his desk that bore slogans such as "Never Trust Atoms—They Make Up Everything," and "We Have So Much Chemistry Together." He was passionate and knowledgeable about his topic, but he was a lousy teacher.

After dozing through many of his uninspired, early-morning lectures, Kaye and I had fallen way behind in our understanding of the content. Hearing echoes of our parents' voices in our heads, we were nervous about our grades on the upcoming test. We knew we had to stay up all night and cram.

Up until this point in my life, I had never had a cup of coffee. Both of my parents were British immigrant tea drinkers who believed in serving whole milk to their growing teenagers. Luckily, I was born a morning person. I usually woke early, was cheerful and bright, and did well academically, even with a 7:20 a.m. high school starting bell. But then came college—no rules, no parents, no sleep. And Mr. Seager. To be fair, Mr.

Seager was not atypical of the teachers at most universities. Their practice was to stand at the front of the room, back to the class as they wrote notes on the board and lectured simultaneously. They handed us ridiculously heavy textbooks to cart back and forth each day, and a stack of mimeographed supplemental materials to complete for homework. With large class sizes there was little opportunity to ask questions when you didn't understand something. This type of teaching was fertile soil for dozing students.

Thank goodness for the 24-hour donut shop on the corner. Kaye and I had been inside several times for warm, melt-in-your-mouth, midnight donuts, but we suddenly realized the shop also sold coffee at all hours. A quick trek from our dorm, and within minutes we were back to our studies with two mega-cups of coffee. My first sip was tentative. I added sugar and cream to smooth out the flavor. A few gulps later and the buzz was palpable! The words on the page began to make sense, connections jumped out at me, and our conversation was rich with comprehension. Sadly, I can only report that we both received Cs, but the caffeinated learning experience saved us from major failure.

Wouldn't it be wonderful if caffeinated learning was delivered up front by the teacher instead? What if teachers, instructors, professors, presenters— all those who facilitated adult learning experiences—infused a jolt of caffeine into their instructional design and delivery? Imagine a room full of awake and engaged adults, interacting with new content in meaningful ways, ready to return to work with the necessary knowledge and skills for successful application. What would it take to accomplish this? That's where caffeinated learning comes to the rescue.

As anyone who has ever had a cup of coffee or a "Dew" knows, caffeine helps to stimulate a sense of alertness and perks us up when we're tired. Caffeine actually changes what is happening in the human brain. Fortunately, neuroscientists tell us that there are other ways teachers can accomplish this same outcome.

One powerful research finding concerns novelty. Neuroscientists have found that exposure to unexpected or novel experiences causes the chemical norepinephrine to be released in the brain. Norepinephrine produces a heightened state of alertness. Presenters who know this can weave novelty into their workshop design so that adult learners are attentive and ready to absorb new information.

Other research studies very clearly show us the connection between movement and learning. Oxygen is essential for brain function, and enhanced blood flow increases the amount of oxygen transported to the brain. Physical activity is a reliable way to increase blood flow, and hence oxygen, to the brain. Presenters who know this can weave movement into their workshop design so that brain function is optimal for prolonged learning experiences.

Caffeinated learning describes the buzz an adult learner experiences when a knowledgeable facilitator integrates this type of research into their instruction. Although participants might appreciate a cup of coffee at their morning break, the true lift will come from the learning activities. With thoughtful design and skilled conducting, all employees will experience rich, robust professional learning.

This book will provide you with the tools you need to conduct workshops that not only keep people awake, but also leave your participants with the knowledge and skills they need to be successful. From the minute of conception, through the planning and provision, these tools will help you:

- Understand the research on adult learning—*Are they just kids in big bodies?*
- Design workshops that engage adults, rather than bore them—*Think "death by PowerPoint."*
- Prepare for the unexpected—*Is that a tornado siren going off?*
- Imbed technology without becoming dependent on it—*two terrifying words: power failure.*
- Fine-tune your presentation with secrets the best presenters know—*What should happen just before the break?*
- Ensure that your participants walk away with the knowledge and skills you want them to acquire—*Not Just Seat Time.*

Terminology

Rich, robust, strong, flavorful—just as there are dozens of words that describe a cup of coffee, there are dozens of terms used in the field of adult learning.

The terms **workshop, class, seminar, professional development activity** and **conference session** have specific meanings in certain settings, and are used interchangeably in others. Generally, the word **workshop** implies that the learning will be interactive, with the leader acting as a facilitator rather than just a lecturer. For these reasons, I will use this word primarily, but will occasionally use synonyms for variety.

The words *presenter, instructor, trainer, speaker* and *facilitator* may all be used to refer to the same role, that of leader of a learning experience. During a six-hour workshop, it is likely that you will assume several of these styles or roles. During an opening, you may be mostly a presenter, while in the body of the day you are likely to act more as a facilitator. In some fields, the word *trainer* has a negative connotation, as if adults will be trained in a manner similar to the pet dog, Fido. I try not to take offense when I hear the instructor in my class referred to as a trainer, but others might. Check with your contact person to find out the term most comfortable to him and his employees. For the purposes of this book, I will most frequently use the words *presenter* and *facilitator*.

Chapter

The Power of Design

Walk into any Starbucks during morning rush hour and you will see a smoothly running machine. Baristas are greeting everyone with a smile, complicated orders are being taken ("grande, half-caf, soy, caramel latte, extra hot for Anne"), money is exchanged correctly and customers are out the door on time for work. Behind the scenes, things run smoothly as well. Stock is replenished, pastries are baked, employees are trained and bills are paid. While it all seems effortless to the casual observer, much thought and design goes into producing a happy, repeat customer.

Thoughtful design is also necessary for an effective training or workshop. By following proven steps (see *Figure 2.1*), your efforts can lead to a learning experience that is smooth, efficient and productive.

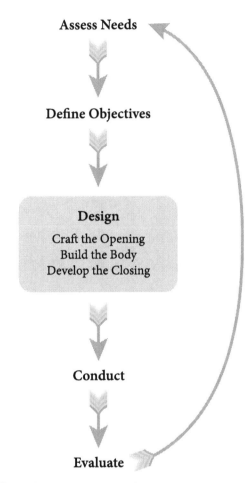

Figure 2.1: The Flow of Professional Learning

Designing caffeinated professional learning begins with recognizing a need and then determining specific objectives that will help you address the need. In certain fields, we may talk about outcomes, end results, or even sales figures. No matter what the field, success will be most readily achieved if we begin with the end in mind. "If your goal is to reach a particular destination, decisions about the route must come after identifying the destination" (Guskey, 2014, p.12). These words from Thomas Guskey, education researcher at the University of Kentucky, remind us that we can't just jump in and begin to decide on the fun, touristy sites and activities of a workshop before deciding where the road is supposed to lead us. Chapters 3 and 4 will take you through a step-by-step process for assessing the need and defining the objectives.

For most presenters, the steps of creating the curriculum and activities are where the fun begins. These are the steps that allow us to feel creative, resourceful and productive. But if these steps are not grounded in solid adult learning theory and research, then they can easily lead you into the muck of ineffective instruction, participant boredom and unachieved outcomes. Adult learning theory and research provide us with valuable direction if we can mine them for concrete applications. Chapter 5 will provide you with the critical information you need about adult learners, as well as practical ideas for how to translate the body of research into your instructional design and classroom practices.

Many research studies have found that the beginning and end of a presentation are more likely to impact learning than what happens in the middle. Impressions and memories are made during those crucial moments. Unfortunately, many workshops have a sense of disorganization at the start and quick, out-the-door chaos at the end. Chapters 6 and 8 will explore a variety of ways to make these moments richer.

But what about the middle? Research points to the importance of the bookends, but can we do anything to increase the value of what happens in between? Thankfully, the answer is yes. By avoiding the traditional "sage on the stage" method and involving participants in a variety of activities, we can increase learning significantly. Pros and cons exist for each instructional method, so thoughtful choices are necessary to boost their power. Chapter 7 provides detailed explanations of these advantages and disadvantages, as well as tips for making activities run smoothly. Chapters 13 and 14 are filled with ideas for technology tools and engaging activities that can be blended to make the body of your presentation richer.

With a carefully crafted workshop design in place, you are ready to start. The thought of conducting a workshop may create feelings of excitement, apprehension, eagerness, anxiety, or a mixture of all of these! The best presenters adopt the Scout motto "Be Prepared," thereby reducing the cacophony of emotions as much as possible before the class ever begins. Simple checklists, reminders, time tips and management strategies will assist you in having a workshop that flows smoothly. Chapters 9, 10 and

11 reveal the secrets of how successful presenters conduct with style and serenity.

Once the workshop is over, you will need to ask yourself—did all the pieces of the process come together with just the right magic? Evaluation is an important part of the design process. How will you know if you have achieved your objectives? How will you know if you have moved closer to accomplishing your long-term outcomes? You may have monitored your audience throughout the day, seen lots of smiles, had several pleasant conversations and heard thoughtful questions. Although these indicators have some value, it will be important for you to design an evaluation plan that gathers more information. Happy surveys can be one tool, but usually only tell you if you were likeable. Hopefully, you already know that about yourself! Commit to a more thorough evaluation through the use of products, action plans and job-embedded activities, as described in Chapter 12.

◎ Key Takeaways

- Thoughtful design will increase the likelihood of accomplishing your objectives.
- Each step of the design process is critical. Ignore a step and your effectiveness will be diminished.

❷ Reflective Questions

- Which steps of the design process am I most comfortable with? Which am I least comfortable with?
- Who might I collaborate with in the design process who has strengths in the areas where I feel least comfortable?

Chapter

3

Assessing Needs

Checking my inbox on January 18th, I find the following e-mail:

> *I am the Director of Curriculum in a small, suburban school district in Indiana. We have a professional learning day for our teachers and staff scheduled for February 13th. Someone recommended you as a speaker. Would you be available to provide us with a workshop that day? If so, please let me know your fee and what topics you could provide.*

Red flags immediately pop up in my mind. Is this day just filler? Do they have any direction? Why is this so last minute?

I know that my ability to be effective as a facilitator of adult learning is based in part on having content that addresses an actual need of my participants. If the boss is simply trying to fill a six-hour time slot with someone who is entertaining, then the odds of making a meaningful impact on their work are pretty low.

What would be better? I always hope that the agency has already done a thorough needs analysis before they call me. Then, in discussions, we decide if the learning objectives they articulate match the expertise I have to offer. But because this is not always the case, I am prepared with a list of questions to clarify the need. As we talk, I quickly evaluate which questions are most appropriate to the situation and add or delete on the fly.

Initial Questions

- What is the mission of the organization?
- What problem are you trying to solve?
- What long-term outcomes are hoped for?
- What specific knowledge or skill is needed? Why?
- What new initiatives are currently being undertaken?
- What are you seeing in work settings that is related to these outcomes?
- Do you have data on current practices?
- What are the training activities usually like?
- Is this learning experience part of a series? If so, is it possible to see prior training materials?
- Is there any unique jargon that I need to know (or avoid)?
- Will there be any elephants in the room that I should know about?
- What follow-up activities will help to ensure application?
- How will the learning be evaluated in the short term? In the long term?
- Are there teaming or collaborative structures that can be tapped to enhance the workshop or follow-up activities?
- What level of acceptance or resistance are you experiencing?
- What are your employee demographics?
- Will participation be mandatory or voluntary?
- Will participants receive any incentives for participating? (credits, time off, stipends, etc.)
- Will supervisors or administrators be present?
- Are break times and ending times flexible?
- Will there be food and drink provided for participants?
- What is the physical space like? How will people be seated? What technology is available?

- Is there anything else I should know before developing the workshop?
- Is there anyone else that I should talk with before developing the workshop?

Spend a few minutes researching your client on the Internet or through conversations with others. Your needs assessment questions will end up being more targeted and productive.

Key Takeaways

- Ask how the needs have been determined.
- Be prepared with questions that will explore needs in greater depth.

Reflective Questions

- How do I currently gather information on participants prior to a workshop or presentation? What works? What do I want to change?
- How can I collaborate with others to ensure that the information I have is relevant and helpful to my instructional design process?

Chapter

Defining Objectives

Picture a seminar brochure in your inbox. In big, bold letters across the top the workshop title reads, "Change is Coming: Are You Ready?" The title catches your eye—change is a topic that affects everyone—so you read on. In bulleted format, the objectives for the workshop are listed as:

- Learn how change affects your stress levels
- Expand your personal comfort zone
- Discover or rediscover your sense of direction
- Believe in your ability to cope with change successfully

These are all things that I would love to accomplish in my life, but they don't make for good workshop objectives. Effective objectives have three critical components. They are:

1. Needs-based
2. Measurable
3. Achievable

First, objectives should be linked to the identified needs of the participants, preferably as assessed through a reliable assessment tool, survey or data. In a tough economy, with limited training hours, we don't have the luxury of addressing objectives that are "fluff" or unrelated to immediate needs.

Second, objectives should be written in measurable terms. Which of the following objectives will be easier to measure?

1. The participant will expand his/her personal comfort zone.
2. The participant will develop an action plan that includes one specific change they will make next week to improve his/her phone etiquette.

Objective #2 is specific enough to be measurable at the end of the day, and provides clear direction for content development. If this is one of my objectives for a workshop, I should be able to show the client how the content of the day lent itself to learning the necessary skills to accomplish this objective, as well as have documented proof that I achieved my objectives. In this day and age, measurable results matter! If I hope to be invited back, if I hope to receive referrals, if I want to feel satisfied with my work, I need to be able to show positive outcomes.

Here are a variety of measurable objectives, with slightly different formats. The common denominator is that terms are specific, observable and measurable.

The participant will be able to:

- Identify five factors that impact student attention
- Create a plan that includes the three components of differentiation
- Using a rubric, analyze colleague interactions for problem-solving skills
- Given the product manual, troubleshoot to three levels independently
- Accurately describe the steps in the process of workshop design
- Given a diagram of a crime scene, locate key search areas for fingerprints
- Choose, adapt and assemble a collection of five tools to share at a staff meeting
- Model the four steps of the Fair Hearing Process during an in-class simulation

Third, objectives must be achievable in the time provided.

My husband, a weekend athlete, decided five years ago to do an Ironman event. An Ironman event is grueling, comprised of a 2.4-mile swim, a 112-mile bike ride, followed by a marathon run of 26.2 miles! Given that he is in his late 50s, it was reasonable for him to develop a five-year plan, with shorter-term objectives for each year. Now that he has registered for the actual event, he might be wishing he had more time! However, the initial objective was accomplishable within the allotted time frame.

It is common for managers and administrators to overreach in trying to set objectives with a presenter. They are hopeful that you will be able to fix everything in a total of six contact hours. Your job is to hold your ground and agree only to objectives that are reasonable enough to be accomplished in the time provided. Rather than being pressured into agreeing on objectives beyond your reach, consider suggesting several days of training over time. Sustained training over the long term has actually shown to be much more effective than "one-shot" deals. This will allow you some flexibility in coming to agreement on the breadth of your instructional objectives.

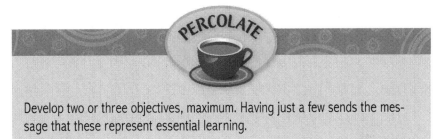

Develop two or three objectives, maximum. Having just a few sends the message that these represent essential learning.

Learning objectives should be clearly shared with participants before and during the event. I often ask participants to reflect on their current skill or knowledge level with each objective and complete a Personal Progress Bar, see page 112. We can then refer back to this throughout the day, shading in the bar(s) as confidence or skill improves.

Learning objectives are essential, but for maximum impact they should be linked to longer-term outcomes. What is the mission of the company or agency? How does the company measure its success? Is there a way to evaluate the training in relationship to these outcomes? Making these links between workshop objectives and long-term outcomes in the beginning will yield greater results.

A suburban school district offered its teachers a workshop on reading assessment. The stated objective was that the participants would "be able to utilize a new tool to assess reading comprehension." At the end of the day, 100% of the teachers had demonstrated the ability to perform this skill. Success? In the short run, yes. But if this doesn't result in improved reading by the children they teach, then the training has been a waste of time. Chapter 12 explores some of these evaluation issues in more depth.

◎ Key Takeaways

- Objectives should be needs-based, measurable and achievable.
- As the workshop facilitator, you are responsible for collaborating to determine appropriate, obtainable objectives.

☯ Reflective Questions

- Have my objectives been needs-based, measurable and achievable? Where is the strength? Where is the weakness? What do I want to change?
- How might I increase collaboration with my client in determining objectives?

Chapter

Adult Learners

Andragogy, the method and practice of teaching adult learners, is based on several underlying assumptions. Malcolm Knowles, considered the father of adult learning theory, and advocate of these assumptions, believed that adults differed significantly from children in several important ways:

- Adult learners have a need to be self-directed.
- Adults bring vast experience to the learning activity.
- Adults learn best when they perceive a need to know something.
- Adults are application- or performance-oriented (Knowles, 1970).

Most K–12 educators these days would argue that students also learn best when we design instruction with these underlying assumptions. Perhaps adults and children don't differ as significantly as was once believed. All learners yearn for independence, respect, real-life connections and competence. No matter what age your audience, these underlying principles are helpful to keep in mind when designing and providing your learning activities.

Adult Learners Have a Need to Be Self-Directed

One word best describes this principle: *control*. Adults have control over many aspects of their lives, and usually want that control to extend to their work environment. As a workshop presenter, you will be most happy when you get to work with a group of participants who have all chosen to attend your seminar. But there will be times when you will face an audience who has been mandated to attend and are not very happy about it. In both cases, your participants will be more open to learning if you can build in some opportunities for them to control parts of their experience.

Ideas

- Let adults choose where to sit, at least at the beginning of the day. By respecting them in this way, you set a tone from the start that they will have some opportunities for self-direction.

- Explain early in the day that they will be able to pick and choose among several ideas offered during the seminar (and then build in these choices!). As soon as participants hear "pick and choose," some of their defensiveness will decrease.

- During the first few "turn and talk" activities, allow participants to choose someone to talk to. As the day progresses and they begin to feel more comfortable, you can direct them to work with specific individuals.

- If role-playing activities are part of the training, develop choices within the task. For example, participants might choose whom they role-play with, which role they take on, what the details of their story might be, or whether they role-play in front of one observer or several.

- For application tasks, such as writing a plan or creating a flowchart, allow adults to adapt the task to best fit their needs. When they see real application to their day-to-day work, they will be more motivated and productive.

Adults Bring Vast Experience to the Learning Activity

While even preschoolers bring experience to a learning activity, adults clearly bring much more. The exciting news for presenters is that this experience, when effectively tapped, will actually help increase retention of new learning. Rather than being afraid of the "expert" participant who wants to share his or her background knowledge, create strategic moments throughout the day when all participants can make connections and share experiences.

Ideas

- Recognize the amount of experience in the room near the beginning of the session. I often say, "I know that I am not the only one in this room who can help you accomplish your learning objectives today. Find someone near you and introduce yourself, sharing what you hope to learn today."

- Encourage participants to make connections by providing them with small, blank puzzle pieces. I cut these out with a scrapbooking tool that I found on the Internet. I ask participants to take 30 seconds of silence and connect a new idea to something in their experience, and write a word or phrase on the puzzle piece to capture it. Then I ask them to work in a small group of three to five people to build a puzzle with their pieces, sharing as they contribute their pieces to the whole.

- Listen carefully for a question that lends itself well to throwing back to your audience. Say, "That's a great question, and there might be multiple perspectives on the answer. Turn and talk with someone near you about your answer to the question. Then we will share some ideas with the whole group."

Adults Learn Best When They Perceive a Need to Know Something

Do you know any teenagers who question their need to learn algebra? Perhaps you did, too, when you were in high school. It is difficult to become excited and motivated about a topic that seems irrelevant to your life. For me, that topic was Spanish. There were very few Spanish speakers in my community during my high school years, and I knew none of them personally. The influx of Spanish speakers on the horizon was not yet obvious, and I had no plans to travel to a Spanish-speaking country. Instead, Spanish was simply a required course I had to take in order to graduate. Fast-forward 30 years to an age when I have the time and financial security to be able to travel, and my interest has changed dramatically. I have purchased audiotapes to teach myself Spanish, enrolled in a class at my local community center and sought out "Spanish-only" coffee dates with a new acquaintance from Columbia. I perceive a need or benefit, and now I am ready to learn. As a presenter, part of your responsibility is to help participants perceive a need to learn your content.

Ideas

- Ask participants to brainstorm the benefits of the concept you are presenting. When the benefits are generated by the learners, instead of being listed by you, they have more intrinsic value. (See Chapter 14 for creative brainstorming activities.)

- Design a case study that highlights the advantages of having the new knowledge or skill (or the disadvantages of not having it). Provide participants with a few reflective questions and direct them to gather in small groups to discuss the case.

- Arrange for a short period of personal reflection, followed by a silent writing prompt that begins with "As a result of this class, I will be able to …"

- Before the workshop begins, try to meet as many participants as possible, finding out what positions they hold, why they are attending and what they hope to learn. If you meet someone who is not sure how the content is relevant, help them make connections. For example, I was facilitating a workshop on co-teaching between special education teachers and general education teachers. The school had decided to send everyone, including P.E. teachers, librarians and choir directors. As it was highly unlikely that these individuals would ever co-teach, I told them that throughout the day I would weave in teaching strategies that they would be able to use in their unique settings. Then I made sure to do so!

- In discussions with your contact person, gather key information that will help you assess whether participants perceive a need for this learning experience. If not, who is it that perceives the need?

Adults are Application- or Performance-Oriented

Immediate application of a new skill increases the likelihood of retention. Adults understand this intuitively, and appreciate learning opportunities that allow for this. Unfortunately, most workshop formats make it difficult to arrange real-life application exercises. If you have been hired to provide job-embedded coaching, the picture brightens tremendously. But for the more traditional seminar or workshop sessions, the good news is that there are strategies you can employ to simulate application experiences.

Ideas

- Role-playing, a dreaded term to most adults, is an effective method for practicing new skills. Proactively prevent the groan by calling it an "application exercise" or "simulation." To reduce stress further, model it first, and then build some choices into the simulation so that the participants feel in control. My favorite simulation structure is to place participants in trios, with two people actively engaged in the role-play, while the third acts as an observer. The roles rotate, so that eventually all three people have had the opportunity to practice the skill and receive feedback. Provide a simple observation rubric to ensure that the feedback is based on the skills you have identified as necessary.

- Show a video of the skill you are teaching. Ask participants to evaluate the individuals in the video with a simple rubric. Share responses through live discussion or through backchannel chat rooms like TodaysMeet.com. (See Chapter 13 for more technology tools.)

- If technology is available, use one of the fabulous online animation tools to have participants develop an animated version of their learning. GoAnimate.com allows up to ten lines of text per animation for free, with an unlimited number of animated videos. If you need something longer, there are several tools that can be purchased at a reasonable cost.

- Build time into the day for participants to develop a detailed action plan that they will implement immediately upon returning to work. Provide an action plan form that prompts them to list specifics (what, when, how) and an assessment component, i.e., "What evidence will I collect to show I achieved my objectives?"

Memory and Retention

Another popular learning theory was posed by Edgar Dale, an education professor at Ohio State University in 1946. As part of his work there, he developed the Cone of Experience to suggest that different teaching methods resulted in different levels of retention (see *Figure 5.1*). Information shared purely through lecture would lead to minimal results, while learning experiences that included immediate application yielded the highest results. At some point in the 1940s, an unknown person added specific percentages to the Cone of Experience and the graphic morphed to include these numbers (see *Figure 5.2*). Since that time, it has been included in lectures, articles, books and slides as "research" rather than theory. In fact, an exhaustive Internet search, along with several letters of query, led me to find absolutely no valid research to support these numbers.

Level of Retention

Figure 5.1: Dale's Cone of Experience

Level of Retention

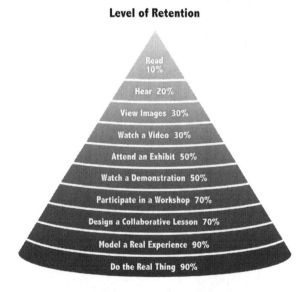

Figure 5.2: Dale's Cone of Experience Adapted

Do these percentages make common sense? Yes. But instead of relying on undocumented data, let's explore some actual research that supports Dale's theory.

Author and educator Marilee Sprenger is an expert on memory research. In her book *Brain-based Teaching in the Digital Age*, Sprenger (2010) explains that we all have multiple memory paths, just as there are multiple aisles in your local market. We can spend all day walking up and down the cereal aisle looking for carrots, but we are never going to find them there. Similarly, if we store memories in our brain using one of the memory systems, we are going to have to find it using that same memory system. It is only when we begin to store memories by using multiple memory systems that we can access them in a variety of ways.

Like Cone's belief that different teaching approaches yielded different results, memory experts have identified five memory systems, each with unique features and results.

1. *Episodic memory*, sometimes referred to as location-driven or contextual, provides a link between the "what" and the "where" of your learning experience. Effective facilitators apply this by using specific areas of the room to make specific points. The learning is linked to the location and becomes easier to remember.

2. *Automatic memory*, or conditioned response, is being used at this very moment as you are reading these words. You are not sounding out every letter, but automatically recalling the words. Music is closely associated with automatic memory because of its ability to trigger strong memories with just two or three notes. Facilitators can tap into this with activities such as rhythmic chants, musical cues and repeated practice.

3. *Semantic memory* is language-based; everything we learn primarily through words is stored in this system. Traditional instruction relies heavily on the semantic system. Unfortunately, researchers believe that multiple semantic repetitions are needed in order for long-term storage to occur. Successful facilitators blend memory paths to make retention easier. For example, to teach new terminology, a presenter might sit down in the middle of the audience and tell an emotional story that incorporates the keywords.

4. *Procedural memory* keeps you from falling over on your bike (once you've learned how to ride without your training wheels!). Often referred to as muscle memory, this system likes repetitive

procedures. Many of these involve tactile and kinesthetic input—typing, driving and locking the door. Procedural memory is also involved in intellectual procedures such as long division and indenting paragraphs. Facilitators can tap this memory path by having participants complete graphic organizers or, better yet, build things.

5. *Emotional memory* stores experiences that are associated with strong feelings. Because of where this happens in the brain, the emotional memory takes precedence over all other systems. Positive or negative emotions can then interfere with our abilities to store or access other information. Dynamic facilitators reflect varied emotions in their tone of voice, word choice, facial expressions and gestures.

To maximize retention, facilitators should plan learning activities that utilize several memory paths. Compare the two approaches below and determine how many paths are being utilized in each. Which will lead to better retention?

A. To teach key terms, Jack developed a slide show with definitions and striking photographs, and then told anecdotes about each term. He asked participants to move to wall charts and work with others to draw symbolic representations of each term.

B. To teach key terms, Jill developed a handout for participants to follow as she lectured about the word definitions. She left blanks for everyone to complete, and then had partners quiz each other on the word meanings.

Jack provided a greater variety of paths to learning and enhanced memory. Though each presenter will have his or her own special blend of activities, the most robust retention happens when multiple memory paths are triggered.

Long-Term Outcomes

In Douglas Reeves' book, *Transforming Professional Development into Student Results* (2010), the author summarizes the research on effective professional development into five key factors. While the research reflects what is known about success in K–12 school districts, other fields can benefit from the results.

1. *Focus*. The district or agency should have a clear focus for learning, without spreading itself too thin. Rather than providing workshops

on a dozen different topics within a year, success comes from choosing a few major areas for improvement and then wisely allocating resources in those select areas. With this approach, employees perceive a commitment on the part of management, the workshops can become more intense, and the necessary support is allocated to ensure success.

2. *14+ Hours*. A synthesis of research done by Darling-Hammond and Richardson (2009) shows that professional development activities on a single topic that last less than 14 hours are unlikely to result in a significant improvement in outcomes. This means that a one- or two-day workshop, if not followed up with other types of learning activities, is probably a waste of time and money. Many presenters are uncomfortable with this research, as it may call into question their purpose. However, workshops can continue to serve an important purpose as long as they are part of a long-term plan with varied activities.

3. *Job-Embedded*. "Now I get it!" are the words I often hear during job-embedded professional development. This "aha" moment is rare during a workshop, but common when learning takes place on the job, in the context where it is most needed. As participants begin to apply the skills they learned in the training, deep, contextual thought can occur. Professional problem solving with colleagues yields solutions that are more realistic than first developed in the conference room. Differentiated assistance can be provided as the facilitator and the learner begin to recognize unique strengths and weaknesses.

4. *Deliberate Practice*. More than 10,000 "twinkles" were heard in our house as my daughter learned to play classical guitar beginning at age five. Her deliberate practice, at times tedious, led her to acquire solid skills as a musician. Malcolm Gladwell, in his popular book Outliers (2008) recounts dozens of examples of how people who are successful in their field got there by practicing the necessary skills over and over again. Adults who want to learn anything well (and the instructors who want the same thing) need to arrange opportunities to practice, with gradually decreasing guidance.

5. *Feedback and Application*. There is an old adage: "Practice doesn't make perfect; practice makes permanent." Practice without feedback may lead to wonderful results or hard-to-break bad habits. In order for practice to yield the best results, feedback is essential. Reeves

suggests that feedback be "low-risk, frequent and constructive" so that the adult learner can form new habits in line with the job requirements (2010, p.59). If feedback is frequent, it will prevent poor practice from becoming habit. Feedback should be specific and constructive. "Your writing style just doesn't cut it" is not nearly as helpful as "When you used these words in the e-mail, they caused some confusion. What are some ways you could reword this? Do you use the grammar check and thesaurus tools?" Suggestions, when constructive, become a follow-up learning opportunity.

The Power of Variety

Take a moment to reflect on your attention as you have been reading this chapter. Has your mind wandered? Have you been multitasking? Have you had to go back and reread?

Many educators and pundits are concerned about an apparent decrease in attention span. Blamed on video games and television, it is assumed that younger generations no longer have the ability to concentrate for long time periods. So used to rapidly changing images, unlimited channels and sensory overload, their demand for fast-paced entertainment, even in the world of work, seems inevitable.

Marc Prensky, the originator of the terms "digital native" and "digital immigrant" doesn't believe that the young workers of today have an inability to concentrate. Instead, in his book *Brain Gain: Technology and the Quest for Digital Wisdom*, Prensky points out, "People's attention spans depend—and have always depended—very much on what they are doing and how they feel about it" (2012, p. 72). As far back as the nineteenth century, the German philosopher Friedrich Nietzsche cautioned, "Against boredom even the gods themselves struggle in vain."

Neuroscience is rapidly adding research to our understanding of attention. Judy Willis, author, teacher and neurologist, applies the latest neuroscience to the world of education, providing practical tips on how teachers and presenters can ramp up learning. Willis describes how key neurotransmitters in the brain decrease significantly after about 20 minutes of engaging in one type of activity. Within seconds of switching activities—from listening to a lecture to talking with a peer, from watching a video to standing in response to a question—the neurotransmitters replenish themselves to more optimal levels. These "syn-naps," or brain breaks, prevent overload during extended learning sessions (Willis, 2007).

Instructors who want caffeinated learning—learning that engages and lasts—must stay apprised of the latest theory and research and infuse it into their workshop design.

Place a coupon for a door prize under someone's chair before participants arrive. When you sense a need for movement, ask everyone to check under their chairs to find the winning ticket!

◎ Key Takeaways

- Honor what the adult learner brings into the classroom.
- To increase long-term retention, it is essential to use a variety of instructional methods.

☯ Reflective Questions

- In what ways do I currently honor my adult learners' experiences and knowledge? Based on this chapter, how do I want to change my practices?
- How might I change my workshop design to increase long-term retention?

Chapter

6

Workshop Design:
Crafting the Opening

My father worked his way up in the retail industry from sales clerk to store manager, all without any college experience. What he did have was a strong work ethic and a keen sense of how to interact with others. I remember many lessons he drilled into my siblings and me as we were growing up, but especially this one: "You never get a second chance to make a first impression." This holds true in many circumstances, but particularly so for a presenter meeting his audience for the first time. You have one and only one chance to make your first pitch. Daniel Pink, in his popular book, *To Sell is Human*, tells us "The purpose of a pitch … is to offer something so compelling that it begins a conversation, brings the other person in as a participant, and eventually arrives at an outcome that appeals to both of you" (2012, Ch. 7, para. 12).

If the opening moments are so important to the final outcome, what should you do and how should you do it? A good opening does three things:

1. Grabs attention
2. Sets the tone
3. Introduces the objectives directly or indirectly

A *great* opening does the above three things in a way that engages the learner and makes them want to participate in the experience!

Unfortunately, many workshops begin with what I call the "holler and hush": someone raising his or her voice to settle everyone down, then continuing with a boring list of titles, degrees and accomplishments. Next come the objectives and agenda, eventually arriving at the restroom announcements. Sound familiar? What kind of impression does it leave on you? How else can we handle these administrivia without negatively impacting our first moments?

Ideas

- Whenever you have the opportunity, arrange for someone else to quiet down the audience and review details such as coffee and restrooms. After these details, allow the person to introduce you. Many presenters shy away from being introduced, feeling more comfortable telling their own story. They worry that it seems pretentious. It is not pretentious; it's smart. Another person can establish your credibility in a way that is difficult to do for yourself. Another person can laud you for all you have accomplished, letting the audience know how lucky they are to have you as their speaker for the day. You stand nearby, looking humble, ready to begin with an attention-grabbing opening. To make the most of an introduction, prepare a simple bio that highlights the points you feel are most critical for your audience to know about you, and carry a few printed copies with you.

- If you do not have someone available to introduce you, there are several ways to get the session rolling without the traditional "holler and hush." If you are using a slide presentation, you can advance to a slide that captures the group's attention and indicates that something is about to happen. You might also choose to have a countdown timer projected onto your screen that rings or sings when it is time to start. If you are playing music as participants arrive, turn the music up slightly and then suddenly off. This serves as a cue that you are ready to begin.

- Instead of introducing yourself immediately, delay those details for a few moments. Begin instead with a well-chosen opening—a relevant anecdote, an inspiring quote, a startling statistic connected to your topic—and then weave in a chance to tell a few facts about yourself.

Make your bio more interesting by sharing a few photos, a word cloud (see Chapter 13 for details on Wordle.net or Tagxedo.com) or a brief video clip. Share only the most critical facts that will establish your credibility with the audience and begin to develop a rapport.

• Printed or projected agendas can reduce the time spent with boring details. Keep your agenda simple: a few words to represent a time block. Most participants just want to know "When's lunch?" and "When can I expect to be on the road?"

Tease your audience with a promise of something special in the last ten minutes of the session—"At the very end of the day I will share with you the most innovative idea I used this year." This will decrease the number of early leavers.

Opening Options

Here are just a few of the simple ways that you can grab attention and set the tone for your session:

• Relevant quote
• Evocative photo
• Incomplete definition or simile
• Provocative question
• Unusual prop
• Short story
• Guided visualization
• Audience polling
• Personal anecdote

◎ Key Takeaways

• Don't start your session with administrivia. Choose an opening that will grab attention and set a tone for the day.

② Reflective Questions

- How have I opened past presentations? What worked? What do I want to change?

- What tone do I want to set for my workshops? Will it be consistent or likely to change? What do I want participants to feel/think/know about me as their facilitator?

Chapter

Workshop Design:
Building the Body

Once you have gotten off to a great start, you will want to keep the momentum going throughout the day. Portions of your workshop may include the traditional "stand and deliver" method, but it is critical to vary the learning experiences for maximum effect. Judy Willis, neuroscientist and educator, suggests that learners need "syn-naps"—brief brain breaks—every 20 minutes in order to keep the neurotransmitters at optimal levels for learning and retention (Willis, 2007). This doesn't mean that participants need to stop learning, but instead experience a switch in activity so that they are using different areas of the brain. If you have been lecturing with slides for 15 minutes, insert a brief video clip. If participants have been talking in small groups for 20 minutes, switch to a silent reading or reflection activity. By planning the day to include a wide variety of activities, your participants will stay energized and be more able to process a large amount of information.

Delivery Methods

It's likely that there are dozens of methods for delivering your content. Let's explore the most common ten, with advantages, disadvantages and tips for maximizing their effectiveness. Your job is to pick and choose the ones that form your own special blend of caffeinated learning.

1. Case Studies

Advantages—Case studies are a wonderful way to examine issues when real application experiences are unavailable. They are not too threatening because they ask participants to explore what is happening to strangers (fictional characters), thereby becoming a safe gateway into uncomfortable topics. They can also be customized to closely reflect the specific circumstances you want participants to explore.

Disadvantages—Case studies have a reputation for being boring, and can cause a groan from your audience if that has been their experience. Case studies do not need to be boring! However, they can be very time-consuming to prepare, especially if you are diligent about developing a case that has all the right components and spice for your content.

Tips

- Look online to find case studies that others have shared. You may need to adapt it a bit to fit your needs, but it will save you time over starting from scratch.

- Prepare for the fact that you will leave out some minor detail from your case study that a participant will ask about ("In what city does he live?" "How many children does she have?" "What's his favorite food?"). As you distribute the case study, tell the audience that if they believe a fact is missing, they should just make up the detail themselves.

2. Games

Advantages—Games immediately bring the fun factor into your day. As long as the competition is inconsequential, participants will experience a boost in energy without simultaneously experiencing a boost in anxiety.

Disadvantages—Some adults claim to dislike games, perhaps because they are intimidated or worried about embarrassment. Depending on your topic, games may be an inappropriate vehicle for learning. Environmental education? Yes, use a game. Teen suicide? Try another method.

Tips

- Build a game that includes choices for participants. Choices will decrease some of the possible anxiety adult learners may bring to the situation.

- If the game is competitive, keep the prizes inconsequential: applause, a standing ovation, chocolates, imaginary points or first in coffee line at break. I once witnessed a nasty argument erupt at a seminar after a winning team was awarded valuable gift cards.

3. Individual Reflection

Advantages—Silver, Strong and Perini (2007) list the ability to reflect on one's learning progress as one of the most important skills a learner can have. Quiet reflection time, whether written or contemplative, private or shared, allows the learner to apply the new information to their prior knowledge and experiences, thus making stronger long-term connections. These benefits are enough to make reflection a key component of any training, but one more advantage takes this delivery method to the top of the list: no prep!

Disadvantages—The only way to accurately assess that participants are being reflective is to have them share their thoughts with you or others. Some adults may hesitate to reflect as deeply and personally if they know they will have to share.

Tips

- Develop a slide or other visual that gives everyone explicit directions about their reflective task. Limit reflection time to five minutes or less, and provide a gentle warning as your time frame is coming to a close.

- When possible, allow adults the option to share their reflection verbally, in writing or not at all.

4. Lecture

Advantages—Lecture is a quick way to disseminate a large amount of information and expertise. It can be spontaneous, with no prep, or it can be more organized, with visual supports. The presenter controls the flow of information and participants usually find the lecture method nonthreatening.

Disadvantages—Engagement levels decrease the longer the lecture continues, reducing retention of information. Lecture does not honor the experience adults bring to the classroom, nor does it provide opportunity for practice or application.

Tips

- Pepper your lecture with audience involvement by asking for a show of hands, for a choral reading of a slide, or for participants to stand in response to a question. Each of these quick responses requires no preparation, and provides a quick break from the lecture format.
- Use slides or other visual aids to strengthen your points. Props can grab attention in unique ways. Imagine tossing a football to an audience member when you want to make a point about nonverbal communication. How might you use a basket of assorted fruits to talk about diversity? Allow yourself to be creative in the use of everyday props!

PERCOLATE

Choose two or three words or phrases that will emphasize your key message and use them throughout the session. Words and phrases such as *practical* or *simple to apply* are labels that easily stick and underscore your message.

5. Readings

Advantages—Readings are a wonderful way to bring another expert into your classroom! If someone else has written an article or book that addresses key points in an effective manner, this will strengthen your arguments. No longer are you the *only* one asking participants to make a change. Readings also provide a quiet contrast to a noise-filled day, something many of us appreciate.

Disadvantages—Adults read at different rates. Some will spend time annotating and digesting as they go along, while others will fly through the reading, skimming for main ideas. These early finishers may wander off task or become a distraction for those who are still reading.

Tips

- Ask participants to respect the need for quiet until everyone has finished.

- Provide highlighters, highlighter tape or sticky arrows so that readers can mark significant passages.

- Develop meaningful questions or quiet activities that early finishers can do to fill the moments until all are ready.

Caution—Be sure to familiarize yourself with copyright law as it pertains to making copies of published materials for participants. Obtain the necessary permission for copying, or purchase the materials needed.

6. Role-Playing

Advantages—Role-playing comes as close as possible to application in a real setting when a real setting isn't immediately available. Individuals will have the opportunity to practice new skills, fine-tuning them until they are comfortable and confident, rather than trying those skills for the first time in an important situation that they can't afford to mess up. Imagine if we let pilots test their skills for the first time with a plane full of passengers!

Disadvantages—Role-playing makes most people uncomfortable, especially if someone is observing them. Adult egos can be fragile, leading many adults to put up resistance when role-playing is announced.

Tips

- Because the term *role-playing* has a negative connotation associated with it, change the term! Call it an "application opportunity" or a "simulation," or design a creative theme such as "water cooler conversation" to soften the impact.

- If the role-play will have observers (one observer in a small group is what adults are most comfortable with, but a roomful results in a wider range of reflective comments), provide the observers with a rubric to guide their reflection. Make sure the rubric is custom-designed to reflect the specific skills that are expected.

7. Videos

Advantages—The old adage "seeing is believing" has withstood the test of time because of its inherent truth. Some learners will be skeptical of a new idea until they actually see it working. Other learners will be unable to visualize an experience for themselves; they need to see it to get it. Videos also allow a presenter to bring the real world into a workshop classroom—no need for expensive, unwieldy field trips. Finally, videos are a simple way to add humor to a situation. If you don't see yourself as a Robin Williams-type entertainer, allow humorous video clips to help you out!

Disadvantages—Up until recently, video clips have been a passive experience for the audience. With the explosion of technology tools, it is now possible to make video viewing much more interactive (see Chapter 13, *Powerful Technology Tools*). Any technology use requires a certain level of skill and prep time. Video editing is much easier than it used to be, but still demands some technology chops.

Tips

- Show videos that are two to five minutes in length. If longer videos are required, consider pausing every five to seven minutes for reflection, discussion or some other application activity.

- Prior to starting the video, show a slide prompt that tells people what to pay attention to. For example, if you are showing a video on communication skills, you might set up "Movie Buddies," with Person A directed to note the tone of voice and body language used, while Person B notes environmental factors that affect the communication.

8. Demonstration

Advantages—Demonstrating a skill or process that you are teaching enhances your credibility. How many of us have attended a workshop led by a university professor who has been in the ivory tower for most of his career? Yet if that person demonstrates a specific skill to us, we are more likely to believe that he knows what he is talking about, and that we can do what he is asking of us! Demonstrations help boost the confidence of the learner.

Disadvantages—Many demonstrations require intensive, detailed planning and practice. Without advanced preparation, demonstrations can go wrong, sometimes comically, but sometimes disastrously. When I demonstrate technology tools, I know there may be a glitch as some point during the day. This I can laugh off with a rapport-building comment such as, "Aren't you glad to know that you aren't the only one who experiences technology glitches?" and model how to recover. But if my demonstration goes wrong in a major way—no Wi-Fi connection, the projector bulb goes out and the sound system squeals—my workshop is in big trouble.

Tips

- Practice, practice, practice. In order for your demonstration to be as effective as possible, you want to appear confident and comfortable with the skill you are showing. Depending on the specific skill or process, it may be best to practice it in the actual space you will use for the workshop. This holds especially true for technology. If you do not have access to the space in advance (perhaps because you are traveling from out of town), then arrive early enough to practice before participants arrive. I am always in my space a full hour and 15 minutes before I start so that I can test technology and other components of the presentation without participants watching me.

- Demonstrations can be hard to see in a crowded room. Before you begin, encourage participants to stand up or move to a spot where they have good visibility.

9. Cooperative Group Work

Advantages—Contrary to what some presenters think, you are not the only one in the room with knowledge and experience to offer learners. By building in cooperative group work, you are structuring opportunities for participants to share and learn from each other. What a powerful way to expand the learning for all! During cooperative experiences, engagement is usually 100%, increasing the likelihood of retention.

Disadvantages—Cooperative group work is so much more than "turn to your neighbor and talk about this." It requires well-organized structure to be effective. In most cases you will need to define and assign roles, determine best group compositions, reseat participants, provide a specific task and directions, etc. In other words, prep time! In addition, small group work can feel threatening to those adults who were hoping to quietly hide in the back row or work on other projects on their computers throughout the day. It may take them awhile to warm to the idea of engaging in conversation with their colleagues.

Tips

- Plan your structure carefully based on the outcomes you desire. Is this just a quick reflection and sharing opportunity? If so, then a single slide with a prompt may be enough. Is this a 30-minute shared reading, analysis and rewriting of a document? If so, then role assignments, suggested time frames, and a decision-making structure may be necessary.

- Carefully consider your outcomes in relation to group composition. Will your outcomes be best achieved by having participants choose their partners? Will working with friends lead to off-task discussions or the same old rut? Will your outcomes be best achieved by assigning group membership based on your knowledge of their skill level, attitude, or job position? Remember, as the learning facilitator, it is your responsibility to provide a structure that will most likely accomplish the learning objectives. Be intentional about your grouping practices.

10. Discussion

Advantages—Group discussion requires minimal if any preparation, honors the experiences of those in the room, and provides an opportunity for formative, in-the-moment assessment by the presenter. If questions are arising that you thought you covered, perhaps you need to review that piece of content in a different way. If comments being shared show that the paradigm shift you were banking on has not yet occurred, perhaps you need to add an activity that stretches their thinking in a new direction. The discerning facilitator will interpret discussion and adjust instruction as necessary.

Disadvantages—Shared control is an inherent component of group discussion. Once you encourage learners to question and comment, whether in large or small groups, you are no longer fully in control of what is happening. At a minimum you might find off-topic discussions occurring, or perhaps more scary, you might hear dissension voiced loudly and confidently. You might also experience questions you don't know the answer to, something that new presenters can find very uncomfortable.

Tips

- Provide a specific time frame for the discussion. As the workshop designer and facilitator, be intentional about exactly how much time you feel is appropriate to meet your learning objective. You can always adjust this a bit based on your ongoing assessment of the group, but have a plan in mind and announce it to the group.

- Provide a specific prompt, question or topic that you want participants to discuss. It pays to write this on a chart or a slide so that you don't hear "What are we supposed to be talking about again?"

- If something comes up that is off-topic, suggest the participant see you at a break so that you can give that question your full attention. For tips on handling difficult questions and difficult participants, see Chapter 11.

◎ Key Takeaways

- Shift your method of delivery every 20 minutes.
- Be intentional about which methods will best meet your learning outcomes.

☯ Reflective Questions

- Which delivery methods am I most comfortable with? Why? Which will I add to my repertoire?
- How do I informally assess the effectiveness of my methods as I am delivering the workshop? Am I prepared to shift if my methods are not working?

Chapter

8

Workshop Design: Developing the Closing

Walt Disney once said, "A good ending is vital to a picture—the single most important element because it is what the audience takes with them out of the theater." The closing moments of your workshop are also vital. Thoughtful preparation of your ending can lead to robust outcomes.

Three major purposes are accomplished through an effective closing.

1. Summarize and Review
2. Acknowledge and Celebrate
3. Call to Action

Summarize and Review

What is it you want your participants to walk away with? What were your main concepts, messages, and skills for the day? The closing is your opportunity to hit these one last time, perhaps in a creative, memorable way. A meta-analysis of research on effective instructional strategies shows that summarizing yields significant results (Marzano, Pickering and Pollack, 2001). Spending time here will lead to better long-term outcomes.

Acknowledge and Celebrate

How do you want participants to feel at the end of your class? The closing is a chance to acknowledge your journey together and celebrate their accomplishments. Some participants may have contributed wonderful ideas; some may have experienced significant changes in attitude, while others may have ratcheted their skills up to a whole new level. Whatever the journey, take a moment to express recognition of their participation in a positive way.

Call to Action

The closing can also be a wake-up call, a call to action. Malcolm Gladwell, in his thought-provoking book, *The Tipping Point*, wrote that in order to spark epidemics of change, ideas have to be memorable and move us to action (Gladwell, 2000). At the beginning of the workshop, you shared the instructional objectives, and throughout the workshop you encouraged participants to consider ways to apply their learning in the workplace. This is your very last chance. How can you motivate and inspire them to follow through?

Top Five Things *Not to Do*

1. Look at the clock and realize your time has already run five minutes over the announced finish.

2. Explain that although you have lots more to cover, you have run out of time.

3. Tell participants that they have to fill out their evaluation forms before they leave the room.

4. Say, "We're done," only to call people back together for other announcements by the sponsoring agency.

5. Finish with "If you want more information you can buy my book (video, program, software.)"

Closing Options

Here are a few simple but effective ways to close your workshop session. I often find it most successful to combine two or three of these options. For example, I might lead off with a minute or two for completing a personal action plan, followed by a sharing opportunity with a colleague and then an inspiring quote to bring it all together.

- Relevant quote
- Short, poignant story
- Brief, inspiring video clip
- Celebrity Summary (See Chapter 14)
- Text Message Summary (See Chapter 14)
- Gift Wrap Exchange (See Chapter 14)
- Direct call to action: "What will you do differently tomorrow?"
- Link back to Progress Bars (See Chapter 14)
- Personal action plans (See Chapter 12)

Tie your closing back to your opening for double the impact. This will help participants link all the new ideas together in a cohesive manner.

◎ Key Takeaways

- Don't waste your closing on administrivia.
- Review the most important message in a creative or inspiring way.

☯ Reflective Questions

- How have I closed past presentations? What worked? What have I seen other presenters do for a successful closing?
- What do I hope participants will do differently after the workshop? How might I inspire them to make this change?

Chapter

9

Preparing for the Workshop

An effective workshop begins well before it starts! Planning and preparation may take several weeks, depending on the content and your experience. As a general guideline, I find that it takes three hours of preparation for every hour of presentation when the material is familiar. If I am designing something brand new, it is not uncommon to spend ten hours preparing every hour of a workshop.

One to Four (or More!) Weeks in Advance

As mentioned in Chapter 3, a needs assessment, whether formal or informal, is essential. This first step should occur early enough so that you have sufficient time to interview the key players, analyze your data and begin your design process.

Using the needs assessment or interview data, develop your instructional objectives. These may be collaboratively developed with the agency, or your client may ask you to develop them on your own. Clear objectives will guide your design decisions. It is important to resist the temptation to jump into the creative part of the process prior to nailing these down with specific language. Most of your design decisions (How much time should we spend on this activity? What tone will I need to set here?) rely heavily on the specific instructional objectives. Clarifying these will make the learning more effective and your design process more efficient.

Outline

The next step is to create a general outline for the entire training. Depending on your cognitive style, you might choose to use a web or a more sequential outline. *Figure 9.1* shows a graphic organizer in which I keep the topics broad and do not add the specific activities. This keeps the design focused on the learning objectives, rather than on activities. Once I have my initial sketch, I like to estimate the amount of time for each of the priorities of the training, adjusting so that it fits the available time slot. I may provide training on the same content multiple times to different groups, each time customizing the priorities and the amount of time devoted to topics. *Figure 9.2* shows similar content in an outline style, which may feel more comfortable for some presenters. Finally, we add in the "espresso shots," the activities that will make the workshop more

Figure 9.1: Planning Graphic Organizer

Design and Conduct Workshops

1. Needs Assessment   15 min.
   a.) Questions to Ask

2. Research & Theory   30 min.

3. Openings   30 min.

BREAK

4. Methods/Body   120 min.
   a.) 10 Aproaches
   b.) Integrate Technology

LUNCH

5. Management Issues   60 min.
   a.) Time, Groups, Difficult Participants, etc.
   b.) Butterflies

6. Closings   30 min.

BREAK

7. Technology   45 min.

8. Evaluation   15 min.
   a.) During
   b.) After

Figure 9.2: Planning Outline

flavorful, the participants more engaged. These can be written into your outline or dropped in as you begin to organize your handouts and slides.

Handouts

An effective organizer will flow smoothly into the creation of supporting materials such as a handout and a slide show. Many presenters develop the slide show first, with a paper handout or digital document that is simply a miniature of the slides. This is by far the easiest, most time-saving approach to a handout. However, it may not be the most effective approach for your learners. My preference is to provide a handout that follows the content of my slides in the same sequential order, but includes more detail, prompts participants to complete specific sections, and allows for greater engagement than just the miniature slides. If I know that a paper copy will be distributed, I try to curb my tendency to provide lots of documents so that the client doesn't put a big dent in his copy budget. Digital handouts are clearly more flexible and can include links to other resources that participants might use during or after the workshop.

Slides

"Death by PowerPoint," a phrase that popped up in the early 2000s, has appeared in hundreds of satire videos, cartoons, articles and books deploring the state of slide presentations. While most of the criticisms tend to be humorous, others have claimed more serious outcomes of poorly designed slides. The Columbia Accident Investigation Board, responsible for analysis of what went wrong with the Space Shuttle Columbia, claimed that poor visuals used during a NASA briefing might have deemphasized certain critical concerns (2003). Luckily, most of us are not dealing with life and death issues that depend on our slide design. But if we are passionate about our topic, whatever it is, we want to be sure to follow these guidelines:

- Use photos instead of words whenever possible.

- Choose photos that participants can quickly interpret.

- One photo per slide is best, unless you are intentionally making a point about how several things are linked, i.e., the face of a child, a teenager and an adult.

- Be sure to obtain permissions for photos that are copyrighted. Or, take an easier route and find copyright-free photos on websites such as Morguefile.com and Ookaboo.com. Begin to collect your own photos by snapping pictures of interesting images you encounter on your daily travels. Here's an image that I crossed four lanes of heavy traffic to take and have used several times to emphasize the need for clarity.

- Graphics should also be easy to interpret. The less detail the better. Avoid what Garr Reynolds, communication expert, calls "slideument"—the combining of a slide and a document (Reynolds, 2008). If it is necessary to provide a detailed graphic to participants, do so in a document, and then create a slide that simply refers to the document.

- Explore the use of infographics—simple graphics with minimal embedded text. A quick search will yield thousands of infographics on a wide range of topics, or you can create your own using free tools such as Piktochart, Easel.ly, or Venngage. I created this infographic with Piktochart in about ten minutes.

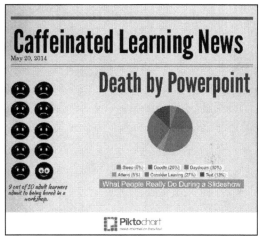

- Text font should be simple and at least 30 point. Choose a font that fits the tone of the topic, and use the font throughout. Alter the font only to emphasize a specific word or idea.

- Follow the rule of fives. Use no more than five bulleted points per slide, no more than five words per point. When possible, avoid bullet points altogether!

- Alternate the color of each bulleted item (i.e. red/blue/red/blue). This allows for easier visual tracking.

- Carefully consider the background color of your slide theme. In a dark room, a dark slide background with white text can work well. However, in a brightly lit room, a white or light background with dark text works better. Because I use slides in a variety of unpredictable settings, I stick with a white background and use text, photos and graphics to add color.

- If the slide corresponds to a page in your handout, insert the page number in the top right-hand corner of your slide so that participants can follow along.

- Avoid using too many exciting transitions and 'fly ins,' as they become a distraction from the message. Use them only to emphasize a key point.

- When using copyrighted cartoons, be sure to obtain permission from the artist. As an alternative, create your own cartoons with an online tool such as Bitstrips or hire a freelance artist through a company such as Elance to develop cartoons just for you.

- Explore presentation tools such as Prezi, Keynote and Haiku Deck as alternatives to PowerPoint. They each have advantages and disadvantages, and are a nice change of pace.

Develop a teaser slideshow—slides with trivia questions about the content—that is set to auto-advance in a loop. Set this to run during the half hour before class to activate thinking before you even start!

Videos

Due to the benefits of video, you are likely to have planned a few video-viewing experiences. Many outstanding videos exist in the perfect format for a presentation, but you may also find that you need to edit some or develop your own. These editing and creation tasks can take an enormous amount of time, especially if you are not a tech guru. Solicit the help of experts if you can! See Chapter 13 for suggestions on simple tools for making interactive videos.

Activities

One of my criteria for labeling an activity a "favorite" is low prep. For thorough descriptions of some of my favorite activities, see Chapter 14. Activities such as case studies also have important benefits, but demand greater preparation on your part. Be sure to plan enough time to generate the supporting materials you will need to make each activity a success.

Details

Send a "Room Setup Request" (see *Figure 9.3*) listing your technology needs and how you would like tables arranged. Ask that your presentation table be placed perpendicularly to the audience. This avoids the "table barrier" inherent to many panel presentations, and makes it easy for you to move around your space.

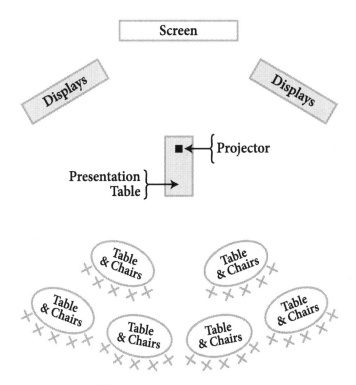

Figure 9.3: Room Setup Sample

Check your handout one last time for layout, graphics and page numbers. E-mail it for copying/distribution at least one week in advance. If your handout is not finished until the last minute, do your client the courtesy of making the copies yourself.

A few days before the session, be in touch with your agency contact. Check to see if he received the "Room Setup Request" you sent and if he has any questions about it. Review the schedule for the day. Is the start time they sent you an actual start time or a registration and coffee time? Ask if break times are fixed or flexible, whether someone will need to take a few minutes to address the group before your start or at the end of the day, and whether you will be introduced. Working out these little details in advance will reduce the likelihood of last-minute surprises. Finally, if traveling any significant distance, I like to have the cell or home phone number of my main contact in case of travel delays.

The following checklists will ensure that you are ultra prepared!

Workshop Checklist

Does the workshop have:

- ☐ Objectives?
- ☐ Tentative agenda?
- ☐ Warm-up/opening?
- ☐ Multimedia?
- ☐ Backup plan if technology fails?
- ☐ Interaction/activity every 20 minutes?
- ☐ Closing?
- ☐ Extra material if extra time?
- ☐ Areas to cut if less time?
- ☐ Opportunity to review?
- ☐ Opportunity for Q&A and discussion?

Notes _____

_____

_____

_____

_____

_____

_____

Trainer's Tool Kit

- ☐ Masking tape
- ☐ Scissors
- ☐ Chart markers
- ☐ Dry erase markers
- ☐ Index cards
- ☐ Post-it notes
- ☐ Noisemakers
- ☐ Playing cards
- ☐ Extra pens/pencils
- ☐ Extension cord
- ☐ Technology cords
- ☐ Name tags
- ☐ Tissues
- ☐ Throat drops

- ☐ Small clock
- ☐ Paper clips/stapler
- ☐ Sticky arrows
- ☐ Music
- ☐ Colored card stock
- ☐ Extra paper
- ☐ Spare batteries
- ☐ Stylus
- ☐ Water bottle
- ☐ _____
- ☐ _____
- ☐ _____
- ☐ _____
- ☐ _____

One to Two Hours Before

No matter how well prepared you are, it is inevitable that things will go wrong. I try to arrive 75 minutes before my official start time to set everything up, check my technology and be ready to greet participants as they arrive. If you have little to set up, e.g., just a computer, then one hour should be plenty.

Recently, I was invited to present a one-hour evening session to a group of parents on a controversial subject. Because we anticipated that emotions would be running high, I spent an abundance of time collaborating with my agency contact to design a session that would meet participants' needs. Part of the evening included a slide show with important video segments. My contact had arranged for the technology I had requested and we agreed to meet an hour beforehand. When we arrived, there was a large handwritten note on the technology cart that said, "The system will be down for a bug repair for the next 24 hours." We problem-solved, scrambled, and were ready to go with our solution three minutes before our scheduled start time! It is at times like this that I am thankful that I always arrive early. I would rather have time to kill, meeting and greeting, than have to apologize to an unhappy audience for starting late.

Because of experiences like this one, the first thing to set up is the technology. Not only will this rid you of tech failure fears immediately, it allows you to put up a welcome slide (or slide show) and play music to set the tone. Locate the lighting controls in the room. Balance the lighting so that it is bright enough for participants to stay awake, but dark enough that your screen shows well.

Next, attend to any items you want to hang on the walls or put on display tables. A word of warning: some facilities will not allow you to hang items on walls. I have found that Sticky Tack will usually hold lightweight items without destroying the paint or wallpaper.

Set up your presentation table with the items you think you will need for the session. On my table, in addition to any technology I will use, I always have noisemakers, markers, sticky notes, a few door prizes, a small digital clock, my copy of the handout, a water bottle, tissues and my phone (for music). Remember to turn your phone's ringer off! I set mine to airplane mode so that I won't be distracted by hearing it vibrate or seeing messages pop up.

Finally, distribute materials to participants' tables that they will use during the training (e.g., sticky notes, markers, dice). I save these for last so that if participants have begun to arrive, I can greet them as I am putting these things on the tables, doubling my efficiency.

With whatever time you have left, actively work the room, meeting as many participants as possible. Some of you might already be dreading this mingling task, but it is critical to the success of your day. Think of it as "maxi-mingling"—a way to maximize the success of your day. Maxi-mingling means greeting people with a smile, introducing yourself one-on-one and asking key questions. As you do this, you are gathering valuable information, developing rapport and even getting to know where your trouble spots might be. Tailor the following questions to your particular content for maximum impact:

- What is your experience with _____?
- How is _____ working for you?
- How are you feeling about _____?
- What are you hoping to learn today?
- Are you here with a colleague or on your own?
- Would you like me to connect you with someone else in the room who has a similar position?
- What type of technology or resources do you have available to support your efforts in this area?
- What type of training have you attended in the past on this topic?

Secret confession: I am much more introverted than extroverted. I am not comfortable mingling and engaging in small talk with strangers at parties, church functions or conferences. However, because I have seen over and over again the value of maxi-mingling as a presenter, I take on the role with commitment and confidence for the sake of meeting the learning objectives.

Time's up! You've done everything you can in advance to maximize your success. It's now time to settle any butterflies and "wow" your audience with a caffeinated learning workshop.

PERCOLATE

Ask each participant to write his or her first name only on a name tag. This results in print that is large enough for you to read from a distance, so that you can call on individuals by name.

◎ Key Takeaways

- Preparation may take ten or more hours for every hour of time in front of your audience.
- Paying attention to little details (readable slides, the order in which you set up) can make a big difference in outcomes.

❷ Reflective Questions

- What are my organizational strengths when it comes to workshop design and preparation? What are my weaknesses?
- What type of experience do I want participants to have as soon as they enter the room? How can I prepare the room to support that? What is my own best way to maxi-mingle?

Chapter

10

Managing the Butterflies

In a popular *Brady Bunch* television episode from the 1970s, Jan, one of the teenage daughters, is nervous about her part in an upcoming debate at school. She frets about how she will be able to stand in front of a crowd and think clearly. Her dad offers her his advice—"Imagine your audience in their underwear"—with the hope that it will help her to remember that the audience is only human. In more than 20 years of presenting, I have never once imagined my audience in their underwear! Instead, there are three solid steps you can take to decrease your nervousness.

Be Prepared

Most nervousness comes from a fear of things going wrong. *What if I forget what I am going to say? What if the technology has a glitch? How will I handle difficult questions?* The more prepared you are, the less worried you will be about these possibilities because you will have thought through how to handle them all.

The 5 x 5 Rule

Because the first five minutes of a presentation are the most nerve-wracking, they should be rehearsed, out loud, at least five times. This can be done in front of a mirror, or as you are taking a walk, but it is important to say it out loud rather than just think it in your head. Repeated practice will provide you a chance to smooth out any wrinkles, decide where to add vocal emphasis, check your timing and boost your confidence.* Even after 20 years of experience, I still do this for any new opening I have designed.

The Backup Plan

When I first made the switch from using an overhead projector with transparencies to a computer with a PowerPoint presentation, I was very nervous that the technology would fail me (or that I would fail it!). For three full years, I continued to carry a two-inch thick folder of transparencies to use as my backup if something went wrong. Guess what? There were a few times it did, and boy, was I glad to have those transparencies with me. For those of you too young to even know what an overhead projector is, here's a more recent example that applies to almost any technology use: power cords. I carry two complete sets of power cords and adapters with me for every presentation, one in my checked bag and one in my carry-on. In my rush to leave the seminar site and get to my next flight on time, I have been known to leave a power cord behind. Without a backup plan, I would be sunk.

What are the things that worry you most about your presentation? Identify these and develop an easy backup plan. Hopefully, you won't need to implement it, but you will feel much less nervous just knowing that it exists.

Defuse by Design

Worry about a difficult participant can cause even the most experienced presenter to have knots in her stomach. Most of us do not relish the idea of conflict, nor do we want others' learning to be disrupted by one unruly audience member. It is the presenter's responsibility to respond to anyone who becomes disruptive, no matter how uncomfortable it is. By following some proactive steps (think "maxi-mingling"), we can often prevent problems from arising. But in order to decrease your nervousness as much as possible, accept the fact that you may have a difficult participant and

---

* Never read word-for-word from note cards. Jot down a few notes if you'd like, but only glance at them if necessary. Instead, try to speak in a comfortable manner, making eye contact with your audience and moving away from the lectern.

learn tricks for defusing them (see section on Difficult Participants on page 75). Create a mental (or paper) checklist of your top three strategies for defusing a difficult situation so that you can quickly pull it out when the going gets tough. I have several small "cheat sheets" that I keep on my presentation table to remind me of specific strategies or skills I am trying to add to my training repertoire.

PERCOLATE

Feel free to move around a bit as you talk. Using gestures or movement to make a point will also provide a natural outlet for some of your nervous energy.

Relax

Sitting in the dentist chair, I can hear muffled voices and the sound of a drill ebbing and flowing. My dental hygienist tells me to "relax" my jaw and I think, "Yeah, right." Perhaps you have the same reaction when you hear that one of the best things you can do before a workshop is to relax. So, how do you do that when you have just a few minutes, people are watching you and it is impossible to lie down on a yoga mat and visualize a tropical island?

Breathe Deeply

Take three deep, slow breaths. Neuroscientists believe that one of the first areas of the brain to be impacted by extra oxygen is the area associated with emotion. Deep breathing, done in a controlled manner, will calm down your nervousness and help you think more clearly. As an added advantage, it is an undetectable strategy that no one else needs to know you are doing.

Drink Water

Drinking water keeps you hydrated but also causes you to breathe in a more regulated manner. Keep a glass or bottle of water on your presentation table at all times. (I prefer a bottle with a cap rather than a glass that can get knocked over onto my papers or hardware.) If you experience a sudden attack of dry mouth, and forgot your water, try biting down gently on the sides of your tongue with your teeth. This causes you to salivate enough to lubricate your mouth. Another secret strategy!

Stretch

While yoga poses may not be possible or prudent right before you start, some neck and shoulder stretches will help. Find an empty hallway or bathroom stall and gently stretch your neck and head to the right shoulder, chest and left shoulder. Massage your neck for a minute to loosen your tight muscles and tendons. Your voice relies on all these muscles throughout the day and they will thank you for a little tender loving care.

Talk Less

The best workshop facilitators have moved away from "sage on the stage" to "guide on the side," recognizing the many benefits of talking less. The obvious benefits include learner engagement and retention. But another benefit is reduced nervousness.

Ditch that Imposter Syndrome

Research done in the 1970s by psychologists Pauline Rose Clance and Suzanne Imes found that 70% of all people studied reported experiencing the imposter syndrome at some point in their lives (Clance and Imes, 1978). This phenomenon causes a person to doubt their abilities or expertise, especially in stressful situations. Given that public speaking is considered a high stress producer, the imposter syndrome is likely to rear it's ugly head at some point in your presenting career.

Presenters who expect themselves to be the ultimate expert, the only one in the room qualified to speak on the subject, set themselves up for the imposter syndrome. On the other hand, "guides on the side" plan to engage their participants in sharing information and ideas throughout the session, reducing the focus on the presenter. When you are no longer the sole performer in the spotlight, you can relax a bit. You don't have to know it all!

Mini-Breaks

Video viewing, partner discussions, silent reading, group activities—all of these learning methods provide the facilitator with mini-breaks. Even if it is only a 60-second "Turn to your partner and react to that," you have the chance to drink some water, look at your notes for the next slide, take a breath, or make simple adjustments to the original plan. Longer activities might even allow you to run to the restroom, something that can be difficult during official breaks when participants approach you with questions. If you have intentionally built activities into your workshop design, you can calm your nerves by reminding yourself that you will have several mini-breaks throughout the session.

Wandering

Talking less allows you to wander more. Instead of standing in the front of the room with all ears and eyes on you, you can wander around the room, checking in with participants and taking the temperature of the group. As you wander, you are likely to have someone stop you with a question. This question might lead you to adjust your next segment for a clearer understanding. As you wander, someone might stop you and say "This is the best workshop I have attended in a long time!" or "That last idea you shared will really work well for us!" Hearing these comments during the day can boost your confidence by leaps and bounds. Or, as you wander, you might pinpoint a trouble spot—a disgruntled participant forced to attend and determined to remain annoyed. Because you are not the "sage on the stage" at that moment in time, you are free to connect with the grumpy guy, develop some rapport, and decrease the likelihood that he will become an extremely difficult participant.

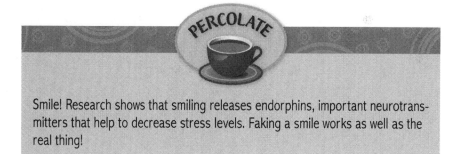

Smile! Research shows that smiling releases endorphins, important neurotransmitters that help to decrease stress levels. Faking a smile works as well as the real thing!

◎ Key Takeaways

- There are concrete things you can do to manage the butterflies.
- Taking the role of "guide on the side" rather than "sage on the stage" will automatically reduce your nervousness.

Reflective Questions

- What is causing my nervousness before a presentation? Have I planned specific strategies for reducing these stressors?

- How might I use my planned engagement activities to manage my nerves? Are there specific methods that I am more/less comfortable using?

Chapter

Conducting the Workshop

The workshop is going smoothly. You've developed a nice rapport with the group, participants are engaged and happy, your timing seems to be just right and then ….

What did you imagine after the "then?" Whatever you imagined, it has probably happened to a workshop facilitator somewhere. No matter how well planned your event, something unexpected is likely to happen. Shortly after the Sandy Hook Elementary School shooting, I was facilitating a workshop in a school in the Midwest. Just before I began, I was approached by my agency contact who informed me that at some unknown point during the day there would be a "live shooter" drill in the building. This is as dramatic as it sounds—gunfire, shouting, police and ambulance sirens—hardly the kind of thing that can be ignored. My group was not expected to participate, and I was told that we could just carry on as if nothing was happening. *Unlikely*. Not only would the noise be disruptive, but it would bring vividly to mind the terror experienced by the children and staff of Sandy Hook. My training and preparation took over. When the shooting began, I acknowledged it and asked everyone to pause. I suggested that we take a break in whatever way each person needed to, and that we would continue with our work in 15 minutes. I knew that I had planned sections of the workshop that I could cut (or add) depending on timing (see Workshop Checklist on page 58). I also knew that intense emotion could aid or interfere with learning, depending on the circumstances. Acknowledging the emotions participants might be feeling and giving time for each person to process those emotions was much more efficient than trying to plow ahead through the content.

How can you conduct your workshop to maximize benefit, even when the unexpected occurs?

Environment

- Notify participants in advance that room temperatures (and tolerances) can vary throughout the day. Encourage everyone to dress in layers for comfort.

- Locate the room controls for temperature and lighting before your session begins. It is helpful to be able to adjust the temperature without having to locate a building custodian.

- Arrange tables so that groups of four to six can work together. My preference is for round tables with participants arranged three-quarters of the way around so that no one has his back to the screen. Allow enough space between tables for you to roam easily, especially to reach the tables at the back of the room.

- If you arrive to find a room much larger than you need for your audience, feel free to rope off (masking tape also works) back rows so that everyone sits closer to the front. As participants arrive, it is also acceptable to request that they sit near the front. When participants are spread very far apart, it is difficult to generate quick introductions and interactions among learners.

- Accept that seating is not always flexible. Do not let fixed, auditorium-style seating prohibit you from asking the audience to turn and talk with others, stand in response to questions or move around the room.

- Use music to set the tone as your audience arrives. My preference is for upbeat, instrumental music—no vocals. I have found that vocal music can be overwhelming and inhibit participants' conversation with one another. Play music before the start, at breaks and after the workshop. Turning your music off is a subtle cue that break time is over.

- Use color to enhance the learning environment. Colored charts, bright paper, sticky dots, highlighters and markers or other materials on tables suggest that a positive, upbeat experience is just ahead!

- If your content lends itself to displays, arrange the display tables around the room so that they are easily accessible. Adults like to explore books and materials relevant to their learning. Work samples, technological devices, products from previous classes—all of these can spark new thoughts and conversation as participants browse during breaks. Develop and place tented cards that describe the materials for participants. This will free you up to answer questions and visit with people rather than be tied to your display tables.

Time Issues

- Start no later than five minutes after your scheduled start time. This recognizes that minor problems may have delayed a few participants, but doesn't annoy those who arrived on time.

- Provide a formal break every 90 minutes, except for after lunch. The ability to attend while digesting is significantly hampered! Plan a break within 60 minutes in the time block immediately following a meal. Avoid the temptation to skip the afternoon break and go right through. If time is tight, shorten the afternoon break to eight minutes, but don't drop it entirely.

- Break when you say you will break. If your agenda lists a break at 10:00 A.M., aim to break by 9:55. Participants will never complain about finishing a few minutes early, but can be unforgiving when held a few minutes late.

- Do not look at your watch or pick up your cell phone to check the time. It is nearly impossible to do this in a way that audience members will not see you. Instead, place a small digital clock on your presentation table, faced in a way that you can easily see it from your primary standing position. As a facilitator, do not draw learners' attention to the time. You want them to be pleasantly surprised at how quickly the time has flown by!

- Your initial workshop outline included estimated time frames for each component of the day. Mark these times in your presentation notes so that you can determine if you are on schedule throughout the day.

- Display a visual timer for group activities and discussions. There are many to choose from: software programs, apps and websites. If you have a reliable Internet connection, you can try www.online-stopwatch.com, a free tool that includes a variety of visual and auditory timers. For the Mac, I use an app called Timer by Ten, and for the iPad I use an app called Giant Timer.

- Use your best judgment to determine which activities may require flexible time frames. Explain at the beginning of the activity how much time you think participants will need, but let them know that you will monitor their progress and adjust the time if necessary. Asking your audience, "Would you like another few minutes?" shows respect for their needs as adult learners.

- Plan what can be cut if your time is running short, and what can be added if your time is running long. Make note of these plans in your presenter notes so that you won't have to decide what to do on the spur of the moment. During the day, it can be very helpful to solicit the input of your agency contact about what to cut or keep. Collaborating to make these decisions will ensure that everyone's goals are met by the end of the session. Finishing a day 15 minutes early is usually a welcome gift, but finishing 45 minutes early can cause problems. Be prepared with valuable filler!

- Do not draw your audience's attention to the fact that you are running out of time. It will only make them feel they are missing out on something important, or cause them to think that you are not well organized. Make your adjustments privately and move on.

- Transitions from one activity to another can waste valuable time if not managed effectively. Using a visual timer (see previous suggestion) will help tremendously. But sometimes, participants are so engaged in discussion that it can be hard to bring them back together. At times like these, it pays to have a variety of noisemakers. I use a harmonica, a slide whistle, a small bell or a clapper to grab attention. The novelty and randomness of the sound causes everyone to stop their conversation and look up to see what is happening. (There are several phone apps such as Epic Xylophone! and Slide Whstl! that serve the same purpose.)

PERCOLATE

Immediately before any break, use a story, a strong visual or an activity that leaves participants on an emotional high. They will carry this enthusiasm into their collegial discussions during the break.

Group Management

- Group membership will be comprised of extroverts and introverts, and lots of people who consider themselves a bit of both. In Susan Cain's insightful book, *Quiet: The Power of Introverts in a World that Can't Stop Talking* (2012), the author describes the "rubber band theory" of personality, in which we can be elastic and stretch ourselves, but only so far. The introverts in your audience may need to stretch slowly to become comfortable with group work. The extroverts in your audience may need to have some structures that encourage them to listen and reflect.

- High-octane professional learning in groups requires participants to engage with one another. To kick-start this engagement, arrange for each person to introduce themselves to a neighbor right near the beginning of the session. The sooner you can decrease the discomfort of sitting among strangers, the quicker your learners will be ready to learn and share.

- Throughout the day, expand comfort zones by asking participants to talk with people who are not seated next to them. If I have a full day with a group, I usually have everyone talk with neighbors in the first morning block, stand and find someone at another table during the second morning block, and then I may purposefully reseat everyone for an activity in the afternoon.

- Group size should be dependent on the purpose of the activity. For personal, reflective sharing, partners or trios work best. For brainstorming, groups of five to eight will generate a long list of creative ideas. For most activities that will require the group to cooperatively produce something, the research suggests that three or four is ideal.

Once your group gets to five or more, it is easy for at least one member to quietly sit back and not participate.

- Most activities will require a group facilitator or recorder. To avoid one group member dominating, randomly rotate roles. This can be done by assigning the role of facilitator to whomever in the group has had the most pets, has driven the farthest to attend, has the next birthday or has the most children. For a twist, place playing cards face down on each table. Ask each person to grab a card. Whoever has the high card (or the low card) will be the facilitator.

- Regrouping participants has many advantages. Everyone will have the chance to gain new perspectives, which is especially important if a major change is coming. Regrouping can also help to break up people who are not working together effectively. If you know the participants well, you can be very intentional in reassigning seats for a specific activity. If not, you can randomly regroup participants by handing out a variety of small candies to each table and asking them to form a peppermint table, a caramel table, etc. Another option is to place a sheet of red sticky dots on one table, blue on another, etc., and then ask everyone to stick a dot onto his or her name tag. Ask them to stand and move to form rainbow groups.

Questions

- Questions are a natural part of a collaborative learning experience. Effective facilitators encourage questions but also need to manage them so that they don't derail the schedule or the learning objectives. Proactively address this near the beginning of the session by telling participants how questions will be handled throughout the day. Perhaps you will have a "Post-it Parking Lot" on one wall. Perhaps you will have a Q&A session just after every break. I usually suggest, "If you have a question today that is unique to you, please come and see me at the breaks. I love talking with people at the breaks, and it will give me the time to thoroughly answer your question, without feeling the group pressure to move ahead. If, on the other hand, it is a question you feel that everyone will benefit from, by all means feel free to ask it at an appropriate time."

- In the best-selling book, *To Sell Is Human*, Daniel Pink reminds us of the importance of listening: "When others speak, we typically divide our attention between what they're saying now and what we're going to say next—and end up doing a mediocre job at both" (2012, Ch.8, para. 26). Try to really listen to the question being asked. You will have plenty of time to develop an answer after they are finished.

- If the question will be addressed at a later point in your content, feel free to politely explain that and ask if it is okay to wait until then. As an alternative, provide a short answer to the question and promise to go into it in more detail at a later point in the session.

- The most dreaded question is usually the one you don't know the answer to. But don't panic! Instead, throw the question back to the audience by saying, "That's a great question. Take a minute and talk with someone nearby about how you would answer it." This allows you some quiet think time, perhaps even the chance to do a quick Internet search, and honors the potential contributions of the participants. If no one in the audience knows the answer, and you have come up blank, promise the group that you will research it and get back to them.

- Occasionally a facilitator will ask the group for questions and none are forthcoming. Before moving ahead, be sure you have waited at least five seconds. Wait time allows participants to process, to decide how to word their questions, to gather their courage. Unfortunately, many presenters are uncomfortable with the silence that comes after a call for questions and move on too quickly. Five seconds can feel like a really long time when you are staring at a quiet audience, but hang in there!

- When someone from the audience asks a question, be sure to repeat the question aloud so that all can hear it.

Difficult Participants

- Know your audience. In Chapter 3 we discussed the importance of gathering data on your audience in advance. Have they been forced to attend your session? Is there anything happening on the job that may cause emotions to run high? Are there any hot button words that you should be aware of (and avoid)? Are there any specific individuals that may be informal leaders and sway the group dynamics?

- Connect with participants you deem potentially difficult as much as possible before the session, during group activities and at breaks. If you can develop a rapport with them, it will help to defuse whatever negative attitude they may have.

- Be reflective about difficult participants. Ask yourself, "Is the person distracting others?" "Is the person disrupting the learning opportunity?" If the answer to either of these questions is "yes," then it becomes your responsibility to address the behavior. If the participant is only bothering you because of her lack of attention (texting, reading, daydreaming, etc.), then it may be best to take a deep breath and let it go.

- Proximity control is a proven strategy, especially for chatty participants. If you notice that a few audience members continue talking when you have begun to speak to the whole group, subtly move so that you are standing near them. Most people will be uncomfortable when all eyes are aimed their way and will modify their behavior so that it is appropriate.

- If a few participants seem to be chatting excessively, they may have an issue they need to discuss. One morning, a small group that was whispering to one another incessantly distracted me. At the earliest opportunity I approached them to find out what was going on. It turned out that one of their co-workers had been in a terrible car accident that very morning. Clearly they needed time to process the experience and discuss next steps. I gently suggested that they move to an available room nearby and rejoin us when they felt ready. When this type of offer is made in a sincere, gentle manner, it honors the adult learners, meets their immediate needs and provides a solution to the disruption.

- "Chatty Cathy" does exist! I met her in a two-day class I taught last summer. She talked almost nonstop to the person on her right or left throughout the morning session. My proximity control, rapport building, pointed eye contact—all did nothing to alter her behavior. At the first opportunity, I checked with my agency contact who confirmed, "She's always like that in a class." During the break, I strategically placed myself in the hallway, caught her as she was returning from the restroom and pulled her aside. I very kindly let her know that her enthusiasm was wonderful, but that it would help me if she could hold her conversation for appropriate times. She was embarrassed, apologetic and the perfect student for the rest of the two days. Remember, it is the facilitator's responsibility to handle disruption. If you need to speak with someone directly, do so in a private place and with a polite, professional manner.

◎ Key Takeaways

- Preparation is key, but you cannot prepare for every eventuality. Adopt a flexible mind-set for those times when the unexpected occurs.

- Presenters are responsible for much more than the content of the day. How the workshop is conducted has a huge impact on how much learning occurs.

❷ Reflective Questions

- Where are my greatest challenges when conducting a workshop? Why?

- How will I prepare myself to be more effective in handling these challenges?

Chapter

12

Evaluating the Learning Experience

The workshop has come to a close, you have packed up your things and you are looking forward to a nice meal as a reward. You stop to take a quick look at the feedback forms and see high numbers. A success! Or was it?

In his book, *Evaluating Professional Development* (2000), Thomas Guskey makes a strong case for discontinuing the use of happy surveys, the typical evaluation form used at the end of the session to determine how happy the participants feel and how much they liked the presenter. These forms usually consist of a 5-point Likert Scale (strongly agree to strongly disagree) and a handful of questions about the day. Only slightly better are the forms that ask participants to write a response to questions such as "What did you like? What would you change about the workshop? What will you do differently based on your learning?"

A well-designed survey can be used to gather helpful data, but should not be the only form of evaluation. In this chapter, we will explore a variety of options, some short term, some longer term, some simple and some complex. Your role as a workshop facilitator places you in a position to advocate for high-quality evaluation that goes beyond the happy survey (even if you don't have the power to make this happen).

Evaluation Forms

Evaluation forms or surveys usually include a Likert Scale from 1 to 5, asking participants to circle a number and write a brief comment. These provide you with quick quantitative data, usually on how happy or satisfied someone felt with the learning experience. One large staff development company found that a 7-point Likert Scale provided them with more reliable information. Generally, it is thought that the more points on a scale, the more reliable the results. However, research is inconclusive. A 7-point scale does have one advantage over the 5-point scale in that responders cannot be neutral on a question.

The most effective evaluation forms have thoughtfully worded statements. Consider the following two statements and reflect on the quality of both. Which will provide you with helpful information about the workshop?

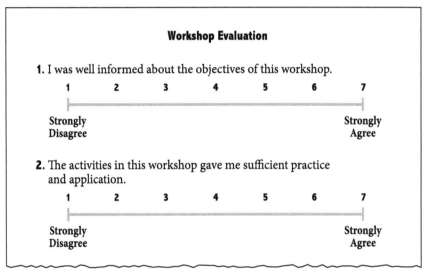

Figure 12.1: Workshop Evaluation (7-Point Likert Scale)

The first statement in *Figure 12.1* is one that the presenter should be able to answer on her own. Did you review the objectives? Were they clear? The second statement can provide valuable feedback on the opportunities for application. Was it sufficient? Did they need more? Based on the scores for this statement, the presenter can make important adjustments to the workshop design for future trainings, and advocate for follow-up activities that provide guided application exercises.

My review of dozens of evaluation forms yielded the following list of questions and statements. Reflect on your needs, choose questions that support those needs or customize your own. Try using different questions for different sessions and use the responses to determine which questions give you the information you seek.

- The workshop activities stimulated my learning.
- The activities in this workshop gave me sufficient practice and feedback.
- The difficulty level of this workshop was appropriate.
- The pace of this workshop was appropriate.
- I will be able to use what I learned in this workshop.
- The presenter was knowledgeable in the content area.
- The presenter's style positively facilitated my learning.
- The content was relevant to my needs.
- The handouts and other resources were useful.
- There was ample time for questions.
- The workshop included ample opportunities for active involvement.
- Examples provided were practical and realistic.
- I gained usable skills and will be able to apply them.
- The workshop was well organized.
- Workshop objectives were stated clearly and met.
- The physical arrangements facilitated learning.
- An appropriate amount of material was covered in the time provided.
- My knowledge and skills in this content have increased as a result of this workshop.

Open-ended questions can provide specific feedback unattainable through a Likert Scale. Consider using one or more of the following questions in addition to or in place of rated statements.

- What did you find most useful about the workshop?
- What suggestions do you have for improving the workshop?
- How will you apply your learning in the future?
- How will what you learned impact your work?

- What did you learn today that you are most likely to try?
- What questions do you still have about the content?
- What additional support would you like to help you implement these ideas?
- Would you recommend this training? If not, why?
- What unexpected benefit did you experience from attending?
- Which of the learning activities did you like most? Least?
- Was there anything discussed today that you still do not understand?
- What was your overall impression of the session?
- How did this workshop compare to recent sessions you have attended?
- What related topics would you like to see addressed in future workshops?
- What changes would you recommend?
- What additional comments do you have?

In-Class Products

Products that are developed during the workshop have two advantages over other forms of evaluation tools. First, they provide the presenter with formative (immediate) feedback on the level of comprehension and skill that participants have acquired. This allows an agile presenter to adjust course, if necessary, to review or reteach essential content. Second, in-class products are highly likely to be utilized after everyone has departed and gone their separate ways. Once a participant has invested time into developing something, his follow-through rate soars. If your goal as a learning facilitator is to bring about change, this is a strong tool.

Your workshop objectives will influence the type of products you might ask participants to develop. If the objective is related to improved telephone communication, participants might create a script or a demonstration video. For an objective about problem solving skills, participants might generate a flow chart or a slide show. The products can be creative, but should always demonstrate the essential skills you want participants to acquire.

As a facilitator, how can you make time spent on in-class products most effective? Consider these suggestions.

- As a general guideline, a single product should not take up more than 20% of the class time. Participants are in the class to learn from you and one another through a variety of activities. If the product will be extensive, break it down into chunks that will be completed as you go through each section of the class content.

- Individuals or groups can develop products. Consider your learning objectives; is teamwork an important component? Or does each participant have unique aspects of his job that he should be practicing? Whenever possible, I like to provide participants with the choice to work alone or with a partner or small group. As discussed in Chapter 5, choices honor an adult learner's need for control and applicability.

- Provide a format or structure that describes the outcome. Outlines, forms, flowcharts and samples are all effective ways to show participants what you are expecting at the end of the work time. If you will be formally evaluating their work, provide participants with a rubric in advance so they can review the criteria.

- Let everyone know up front that you will ask them to share their products with their peers when the work time is finished. Build a brief sharing opportunity into the schedule.

- Roam the room while participants are working, making yourself available for questions or guidance. Notice nonverbal cues that might indicate someone is struggling with the task. Be sure to check in with each table at least once during the work block.

Action Plans

Life Is Change, Growth Is Optional—this book title from Karen Kaiser Clark is extremely applicable to adult learners. Changes in the workplace or life will occur, but not every participant will choose to grow with these changes. If your class has been inspiring, if your instruction has been effective, then an action plan might be the one last thing that a participant needs to follow through with his new learning. Action plans provide a series of steps to guide people as they journey through complex change. Effective action plans have four elements: the task to be done, the timeline, the necessary resources and evidence of the outcome. The plan itself can take several forms, but often looks like the sample in *Figure 12.2*.

As an evaluative tool, action plans provide the facilitator with clues about what was most inspiring, most attainable and most memorable. This

Action Plan

Name_____ Date_____

What will I do?	When will I do it?	What resources do I need?	How will I assess the outcome?

Figure 12.2: Action Plan

information can be used to strengthen specific components of the curriculum or to revise activities. If it appears that everyone has chosen the easiest task possible, rather than challenging themselves with real growth, perhaps the instruction missed its mark.

On the other hand, if participants enthusiastically embrace several next steps, you can relax at the end of the day knowing you met your target.

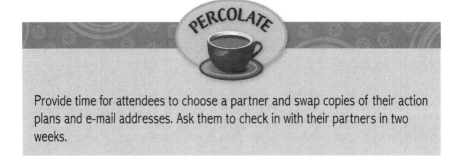

Provide time for attendees to choose a partner and swap copies of their action plans and e-mail addresses. Ask them to check in with their partners in two weeks.

"After" Evaluation

Several other methods exist for evaluating the long-term effectiveness of your training. These are things that take place after the class is finished, although the seeds can be planted during the workshop. Talk with your client in advance about these ideas to see if any are feasible.

After-Class Products

Once learners are back on the job, we want to be sure they can and do apply the valuable skills they learned. One way to encourage application is to require completion of a project prior to issuing class credit. These products provide the instructor or employer with concrete evidence of retention (or lack thereof). Collaborate with your contact to develop project requirements that pinpoint key skills.

On-the-Job Observations

No matter how much effort the instructor puts into designing a realistic simulation activity, the job environment will always be different than a classroom environment. Noise, pacing, and uncontrolled human interactions can all form a cacophony of stressors that cause new skills to fall apart. Observations in authentic environments will allow you to see if the training effectively prepared participants, and help you to identify components of the training that need tweaking. Observations can also lead to the development of a professional learning plan that focuses on an individual's unique needs.

Other Outcomes

Depending on the mission and goals of an organization, there can be myriad ways to link training to outcomes. If the workshop is for a school, did we see an increase in student test scores? If the workshop is for a business, did we see an improvement in customer satisfaction ratings? Perhaps the organization needs to increase sales, find additional donors or reduce accounting errors. Whatever the goal, training should be having an impact. The connection between training and these outcomes can be tricky to ascertain. However, in order to justify the time and money spent on training, it is essential to explore this data.

◎ Key Takeaways

- Surveys given to participants at the end of a workshop can include a wide variety of questions. Choose your questions carefully in order to gather the most helpful feedback.

- Effective evaluation includes much more than happy surveys. Explore a variety of ways to assess the impact of your training, both during and after your event. Learning that lasts won't be evident until your participants are back on the job.

❷ Reflective Questions

- How will I know that my class was successful?
- How might I collaborate with the sponsoring agency to develop a comprehensive evaluation plan?

Chapter

Powerful Technology Tools

The smart use of technology can expand learning in countless ways. By combining strong instructional practices with the power of the Internet, apps on the iPad or interactive software, classes for adults can yield high levels of engagement and learning. With so many tools to choose from, there is something for everyone, for every topic, for every audience demographic. Whether you are technology timid or a technology titan, the ideas that follow will spur you toward greater technology integration.

Because technology develops at an amazing speed, there may be other tools that have arrived on the scene that improve upon the ones mentioned here. Therefore, I have grouped these by categorical topic so that you will be able to search for additional tools to fit these categories.

Reflection Tools

If you are using an iPad in conjunction with your computer and projector, you will want to have software or hardware that allows you to reflect, or mirror, your content between devices. This provides you the freedom to move around the room as you speak, carrying your iPad with you and allowing participants to interact with apps that are simultaneously projected onto your screen. For example, if I want participants to brainstorm ideas about how to adapt a room layout, I might have a picture of the room uploaded to an app such as Educreations, provide some think time and then ask individuals to annotate the picture with suggested changes. If I am reflecting, then everyone in the room can see the suggestions easily. The following tools provide reflection capabilities with different features.

- **Apple TV** is a digital media player developed and sold by Apple, Inc. It is a small network appliance that will play content from any Mac or Windows computer or iOS device. Once connected to the VGA cord running to your projector, and with a few simple setup steps, anything that is showing on your computer screen or your iPad screen will be mirrored through the projector onto your screen.

- **Reflector** and **AirServer** are AirPlay receivers that allow you to wirelessly display your iPad or iPhone on your Mac or PC. With either of these software programs, everything you do on your mobile device is wirelessly streamed to your computer in real time. Reflector also allows you to mirror more than one device simultaneously. With this feature, two participants with different iPads could reflect their work and your image would show a split screen with both iPads visible— great for comparison or collaborative work!

- **Doceri Desktop** is a software program that allows you to reflect, as above, but has a unique feature not currently found in other reflector tools. With Doceri Desktop running on your computer and your iPad, you can mirror anything on your computer screen to your iPad and then annotate the screen. This all reflects back to your projected image. For example, if I have a website open on my laptop, Doceri lets me reflect this to my iPad. Then I can point out features of the website with annotation tools, live streaming this annotation back to the computer (which is connected to the projector).

Backchanneling Tools

Backchanneling is the practice of using networked computers or mobile devices to foster a real-time conversation in the background while a presenter is speaking or other activities are taking place. Backchanneling provides learners with the opportunity to comment on the presentation, ask questions or add ideas, all without raising their hands or interrupting the speaker. Each participant will need access to a wireless device to be able to join the conversation, but most of the chat rooms are free to use.

Participants can even join in from remote locations or communicate during non-classroom hours.

- **TodaysMeet** provides you with a free, private chat room. No accounts, passwords or complicated registration is necessary. Simply enter the website, create a room in under 15 seconds, type your name and send a message. To enter the site, participants use your room's URL and then can share messages with the whole class. Your room can be open for as little as an hour or as long as a year, and all the messages posted are saved during that time frame.

- **Padlet** is a free backchanneling tool that posts comments onto a wall, similar to sticky notes or a bulletin board. Backgrounds and colors add a creative touch that results in a unique visual display. A wide range of settings also allow users to add video, photos or website links to their posts. Boards can be shared through several social network sites while in progress or as finished products.

Audience Polling/Assessment

Formative assessment refers to the ongoing assessment of students' learning progress for the purpose of changing instruction to meet their needs. Effective trainers utilize this data to make minor adjustments throughout the day, or more major changes from class to class. Data can be collected on specific content knowledge or participants' opinions and beliefs. The following technology tools utilize different approaches to gathering data, but all are engaging and free!

- **Poll Everywhere** is a website that allows for instant audience feedback through text messaging or computer use. Just type in a question, either multiple choice or open-ended, and start the poll. As soon as answers are submitted they are displayed on the screen, either in text format or a bar graph. Poll questions can contain uploaded photos, and poll backgrounds can be customized.

- **Infuse Learning** provides a number of response options for your audience, but two that stand out as unique. With Infuse Learning, a teacher can ask learners to draw an image of some kind and submit it for all to view. For example, I might ask participants to sign in and draw a symbolic image of collaboration. When drawings pop up on the screen, the image includes the user's name. This allows the presenter to comment and ask the artist to share her thoughts. The other wonderful feature built into this tool is translation of questions into multiple languages. With a larger portion of our community speaking English as a second language, this translation feature provides private support and makes assessment questions more accessible.

- **Socrative** is a response system that allows instructors to engage their classes through a series of educational exercises and games. Participants can be assigned to teams and enjoy friendly competition as they answer the instructor's questions. Individual responses can also be submitted with multiple choice, true/false and open-ended items. Responses can easily be captured and saved in a spreadsheet.

- **Plickers** are a creative alternative to expensive clicker response systems. Instead of purchasing clickers, print out individual bar code cards (plickers) from the Plickers website and hand one to each participant. On each of the four sides of the plicker is a letter from A to D. Pose a multiple-choice question and ask everyone to hold up his or her plicker. Use a smartphone or iPad to quickly scan the cards, while real-time data shows up as a bar graph on your screen. Plickers also captures individual responses so that the facilitator can identify who may be in need of additional instruction.

Word Clouds

Looking for visually stunning representations of keywords from your content? Word clouds arrange any text into graphical representations, giving words that are used most often prominence in the design. These can be generated in advance or in real time while your participants are calling out keywords.

- **Wordle**, the most popular of the word cloud tools, allows you to tweak your clouds with different fonts, layouts and color schemes. Simply enter your text and click go; dozens of instant word clouds appear in random order. Settings allow you to automatically remove common words such as "the, and, it," so that your message is even stronger.

- **Tagxedo** does everything that Wordle does and more. Text can be arranged into random shapes or dozens of other options Tagxedo provides. Even better, you can import your own pictures that are instantly turned into unique word clouds. You can also import text from a website by entering the appropriate URL. This is a quick way to summarize a blog or other web content. One other attention-grabbing feature: as you move your cursor over a word, it pops up even larger for added emphasis.

- **Visual Poetry** is an iPad app that arranges your text or phrase into a colorful mosaic. In addition to the 24 available shapes, you can draw your own shapes, or pinch and drag to resize and rotate individual words. This word cloud tool is perfect for the artistic presenter who wants one-of-a-kind visuals for his or her slide show.

Interactive Slides and Videos

Are your participants really watching that video or slide? It can be difficult to discern an attentive participant from one who is daydreaming about a beach in Maui. No worries—there are several tools that integrate interactive components to videos and slides. These are a few of the simplest, no-cost or low-cost options that work well for adult learners.

- **eduCanon** is the first interactive video tool that I have found to be flexible enough for using with students of any age. Marketed as a tool for flipped instruction, it allows you to load any YouTube, Teacher-Tube, Vimeo or public video and insert questions at any point in the video. The free version integrates multiple-choice questions and for a minimal fee you can add open-ended questions. In addition to the Q&A, facilitators can include detailed explanations of why an answer is correct or incorrect. Easily set up multiple classes, assign video viewing for after class hours and collect response data. Or watch the video as a group, discussing questions as they pop up.

- **ThingLink** transforms photos from static images into a navigational surface with embedded links. The user can easily tag a photo multiple times to embed URLs that take the viewer to additional, related information. Imagine, as an example, a map of the United States, with links embedded at specific geographic locations that take the viewers to websites with more detail. Up to 50 images can be viewed on a web-based free account.

- **EverySlide** quickly turns your slide show into an interactive experience for your audience. Simply upload your PowerPoint or Keynote presentation to the EverySlide website to get a unique URL that your participants can use to join. At a planned point or on the spur of the moment, ask your audience a poll question or have them add words to an instant audience-generated word cloud. One more feature makes this tool an excellent option for increasing engagement: participants can use their touch screens or cursors to add a heat sensor dot to any spot on the slide. For example, picture a slide with a photo of a work environment. The facilitator could ask participants to place a dot wherever they see potential dangers. The dots can be revealed as soon as they are entered or all at once when the facilitator feels that most have responded.

QR Codes and Augmented Reality

Enhanced content can engage learners by adding an unexpected layer of information to traditional documents or environments. QR Codes and Augmented Reality are tools that can be used in several ways to enrich your instruction. Imagination and a mobile device are the only things needed!

- **Quick Response (QR) codes** are two-dimensional bar codes that are usually linked to a URL. When scanned with a mobile device, this visual code quickly takes the user to the linked content. No more does a user have to type a lengthy URL into the browser, often making errors along the way. Although originally designed for the automotive industry, QR codes can now be found in all walks of life, from realtors' signs to churches to training rooms.

  Easy to generate, QR codes can be linked to expert interviews, demonstration videos, Google documents or content-related websites. Integrate QR codes into your handouts for early finishers, or hang them on the walls to get people up and moving. Scan the QR code below to visit a code generator site that lets you develop codes in color—great for color-coding by groups or content area!

- **Augmented Reality (AR)** is the layering of digital information on top of the physical world. A colleague of mine refers to AR as "QR codes on steroids." With jaw-dropping special effects, AR options are received with enthusiastic engagement by learners of all ages. Aurasma is a popular AR app that makes it simple to generate your own AR experiences or unlock AR content that others have designed. The user begins by developing a detailed trigger image, then chooses an overlay image to place on top. Anyone with the app can then scan the trigger image, and the overlay pops up. Overlay images can include videos, photos, animations, audio recordings, text—anything that you feel will enhance the trigger image. Join my Aurasma channel and scan this book page right now with the app for a simple AR experience.

For workshops, imagine developing an AR experience for a detailed flowchart in your handout. Use the flowchart as the trigger image, then add an expert video interview as the overlay. When participants scan the image, the video will appear in the corner. They can listen to the expert, while still considering the flowchart in front of them. Alternatively, have participants create AR content! First, have small groups develop trigger images of a product they have designed. Next, have them develop digital content, perhaps an audio recording explaining the process they used or the intended applications. Finally, have them link this explanation as the overlay. These AR experiences could then be shared with other groups, supervisors or whoever has funded the training class.

Technology tools are updated frequently. Be sure to perform a dry run shortly before your presentation to make sure that you are comfortable with the latest versions.

◎ Key Takeaways

- Integrating technology into your presentations will engage your audiences in a richer, more vibrant learning experience.
- Technology that involves the audience in creation, rather than just consumption, sends the message that everyone has something to contribute to the class.

◑ Reflective Questions

- What is my comfort level with various forms of technology? Who do I know who might assist me in improving my skills?
- Which of these ideas will I integrate into a future workshop?

Chapter

14

Engaging Activities

Experienced facilitators have a custom-designed collection of activities that they carry—sometimes figuratively, sometimes literally—into the classroom. Sometimes we refer to this as their "bag of tricks." However, this label does the collection and the facilitator a disservice. The ideas and activities in this collection are not tricks. Instead they are well-designed, intentionally chosen methods for engaging learners more actively with the content. A thoughtful facilitator should be able to justify why he or she has chosen to use a specific activity at a specific point in the training.

Over the years I have used dozens of different activities. Some of them worked extremely well, while others were less effective. Some I learned from other presenters who were able to pull them off flawlessly, but they fizzled with me. Not every activity is a good match for every facilitator's style, nor does every activity work with every audience. This is why it is critical to have dozens in your collection to pick and choose from.

On the following pages, you will find 20 of my favorite activities, covering a variety of learning strategies from making connections to summarizing, from building concrete representations to thinking symbolically. These particular activities are generic enough to be adapted for almost any content, and simple enough to need little to no prep time. As you read through them, think of your own content, your upcoming presentations, and be ready to jot notes in the margins as to how and when you will use the activity.

Whenever you attend a conference or workshop, take notes on the content *and* take notes on the presenter's style and activities. Save the best ideas in a file for future reference.

≫ The Back of a Napkin

Many great ideas have been developed on the back of a napkin. Simple drawings can capture the essence of a concept in a unique way that may be more powerful than a paragraph of words. The Back of a Napkin strategy encourages learners to capture their knowledge and ideas in a nonlinguistic representation, using a readily available but unexpected medium.

How To

1. Obtain a paper napkin for each participant. (High quality is not important; often the cheaper napkins, like those found at fast-food restaurants and coffee shops, work best.)

2. Explain that many brilliant ideas and booming businesses have been developed on the back of a napkin. One company that began this way is Southwest Airlines. (For details and additional examples, check out *The Back of a Napkin* by Dan Roam [2008].)

3. Direct everyone to capture their learning by drawing a simple design on the napkins. Words can be off-limits entirely or limited to a few. If desired, demonstrate a few examples with a document camera or iPad.

4. Allow just a few minutes for silent drawing, and then ask participants to share their sketches with one another.

5. Ask for volunteers to come forward and show their napkins using the document camera or iPad.

⟫ Blanket the Table

Blanket the Table serves as a great alternative to more traditional brainstorming. It yields 100% participation, releases a bit of adrenaline to wake everyone up and includes multiple modalities to increase learning. Perhaps the best part for the facilitator is that it requires no prep work. All you need is the back of some scrap paper.

How To

1. Divide your participants into groups of four or five.

2. Provide each person with a half sheet of scrap paper.

3. Direct everyone to rip the paper into four pieces.

4. Ask participants to stand around the table.

5. Set a timer for 1 ½ minutes.

6. Direct the participants to state an idea out loud (a solution, a benefit, a characteristic—whatever your content lends itself to), write it on the paper and drop it on the table.

7. The goal is to blanket the table with ideas in the time provided.

8. When time is up, ask participants to share some of their ideas.

≫ Board Relay

Board Relay is an energizing activity that uses inconsequential competition to engage learners in completing an assigned task. It can be
used across content areas with very little preparation on the part of the
presenter.

How To

1. Divide the class into four relay teams.

2. Review the rules of Board Relay with the participants:
   - No running.
   - No shouting out answers.
   - Marker must be handed to the next team member, not thrown.
   - Winners will be determined based on accuracy as well as speed.

3. Divide the white board into four sections or hang sheets of chart
   paper in four corners of the room.

4. Determine the task for Board Relay. For example, participants might
   be required to list elements or examples of the concept just taught,
   steps in a process and so on.

5. Explain to participants that they will each take a turn in completing
   the task, as in a relay. Depending on the assignment, clarify how
   much should be done in each turn.

6. Explain that finish times will be kept for each team, but that
   finishing first does not mean winning—accuracy is more important.

7. Determine and convey a scoring system.* For example, finishing first
   is worth 100 points; second, 90 points; third, 80 points; and fourth,
   70 points; but for every error the team loses 15 points.

8. Start the Board Relay.

9. Mark the finishing order of each team on the board. When the last
   team has completed the task, engage the whole group in reviewing
   the work of each team for accuracy.

10. Note total scores for each team and try again with a new task.

continued—

---

* Scoring is optional.

Board Relay (continued)

Variations

- Board Relays can be done with partners, so that no participant is left on his own to complete a step of the task.

- Relay teams can be given 30 seconds before the start to strategize about their approach to the task.

- Seated Relay is a variation that reduces the physical movement in the room. For Seated Relay you will need one small whiteboard and marker per team. The participant in the first position of the relay writes on the whiteboard and then passes it on to the next person.

⫸ Challenge Questions

Everyone benefits from engaging in discussion that includes creative, higher-order thinking. It is the facilitator's responsibility to ask questions that stimulate this kind of thinking while keeping it light enough that the session doesn't become bogged down. Challenge Questions provide facilitators with readily available questions, incorporate a tactile medium and include a touch of unpredictability that will keep participants interested.

How To

1. Make a single copy of the Challenge Questions provided on the following page.

2. Cut the paper so that each question is separated.

3. Place the questions into a small paper bag.

4. At an appropriate point in the session hand the bag to a participant and ask him to pull out a question and read it aloud.

5. Tell everyone to turn to their neighbor and develop an answer. After about 15 seconds, facilitate sharing of answers with the whole group.

6. Return the Challenge Question to the bag for future use.

Variations

- Place each challenge question in an envelope. Mark the envelopes with brightly colored question marks and hang them on the walls around the room. At an appropriate time, ask someone from the audience to go to any envelope, pull out the question and read it aloud.

continued—

If you were to have a bumper sticker on your car about this concept, what would it say?

If you were a politician, how would you campaign on this issue?

If this concept was a store in the mall, what would it be called and what would you buy there?

If you were creating a web page for this concept, what would it look like?

Given a million dollars, how would you use this information to benefit society?

If you were to design a reality TV show based on this concept, what would it be called and what would it be about?

If this concept was a flavor of ice cream, what would it be, and would it be chunky or creamy? Why?

If this concept was a song, what genre of music would it be and what title would you give it?

If this concept was a sport, what would it be called and how would it be played?

If this concept was a zombie, what would you do to destroy it?

If this concept was a dinner menu, what would be the appetizer, main course and dessert?

If this concept was a street, where would it begin and end? What streets would branch off of it?

⟫ Celebrity Summary

Summarizing and reviewing content does not have to be dull! The Celebrity Summary activity encourages participants to use their creativity to review key points from the learning. As each group shares its summary, the entire audience hears the concepts repeated multiple times.

How To

1. Make up Celebrity Summary cards by copying the next page, or develop your own and include other celebrities. Cut apart and laminate the cards for durability. You will need a minimum of one card for every four people in your class.

2. Have your participants form small groups—three to four works best.

3. Have someone in each group choose a card without looking.

4. Provide participants with three to five minutes to develop a summary of the content from the celebrity's perspective.

5. If desired, provide an example such as:

   From Dr. Seuss (in a class on differentiated instruction)

   Differentiation is easy, don't you see

   Stand up, sit down, manipulate with me

   Wikki Stix, sticky dots and HOT questions on the wall

   We do our best to include them all!

Variation

For a no-prep version, simply ask your audience to suggest the names of several celebrities. Write them on a chart or project them onto your screen. Tell groups to choose one and develop a summary from that person's point of view.

continued—

You are invited ...

... to summarize
this information
as if you were
Maya Angelou

You are invited ...

... to summarize
this information
as if you were
Dr. Seuss

You are invited ...

... to summarize this information as if you were **Albert Einstein**

Photo by Orren Jack Turner (Library of Congress)

You are invited ...

... to summarize this information as if you were **Steve Jobs**

Photo by Matthew Yohe (Wikimedia Commons)

⟫ Choral Reading

Perhaps one of the simplest of engagement strategies, choral reading has several benefits. For learners, reading aloud as a group increases likelihood of retention and can bring the group to a common focal point. For facilitators, it is a low-prep strategy that can be added into any presentation content to mix things up a bit. However, use this strategy sparingly. If overdone, it may cause adult learners to feel like they are back in elementary school.

How To

1. Choose a short sentence or phrase that is worth emphasizing. It might be part of a longer quote or chunk of information.

2. Prepare a slide in your presentation that includes this phrase, and highlight it with color or a change in font.

3. Read the statement to your audience, and then say, "Read those words in <u>red</u> with me. Here we go ..."

>> Dynamic Responses

Lecturing for short periods of time can be an effective and efficient way to transmit information, *if* participants remain engaged. Dynamic responses can be woven into a lecture, either through planned inserts or on-the-spot decisions. Be sure to use a variety so that the response is novel. I find that if I have a 20-minute lecture block, I will use one or two dynamic responses at some point during that time. I usually model the physical actions as I am asking participants to respond.

- Thump your heart if ...
- High-five or fist-bump your partner ...
- Stand up if ...
- Raise your hand if ...
- On a scale from 1 to 5 show me with your hand how you feel ...
- Give me a thumbs up or down ...
- Stomp your feet if ...
- Say "Yes" if ...
- Applaud if ...
- Give me a drum roll ...
- Wave your arms wildly if you like ...

≫ Gift Wrap Exchange

Sharing ideas is similar to gift giving. To encourage participants to share their gifts, and to value the input of all, use the Gift Wrap Exchange activity near the end of your time together. This activity has a very positive feeling to it and fits in well with a celebration.

How To

1. Buy a roll of non-holiday wrapping paper.

2. Cut it into small pieces, approximately 4" x 4".

3. Store the papers inside a book to help them flatten out.

4. Pass gift wrap to all participants and ask them to write an idea (an inspirational thought, a message of encouragement, etc.) on the back side of the gift wrap.

5. Explain that when they finish they should fold up the paper as if they were wrapping a gift box.

6. Ask everyone to stand and connect with someone else in the room, swapping their gifts before returning to their seats.

⟫ Group Graffiti

Group Graffiti is a quick, creative way to awaken prior knowledge or reinforce new learning. Like graffiti (also known as tagging), thoughts or ideas are expressed in simple but bold artistic messages. The visual display is an appealing alternative to other brainstorming activities.

How To

1. Hang chart paper on the walls around the room. You will need approximately one sheet for every six participants. Place markers on each table.

2. Explain to participants that they will be "tagging" or making graffiti about the lesson topic on the butcher paper. Remind everyone that graffiti usually consists of simple visual images or words, often symbolic. Add that they will be working on the walls so that the different plane will spark their creativity.

3. Have everyone grab a marker and move to a chart on the walls.

4. Write the topic (one to three words) in large print in the middle of each paper.

5. Direct participants to use their markers to quickly tag the paper with anything they can think of about the topic. For example, if the topic was "problem solving," participants might tag words such as "tough, process, collaborative, dynamic" or draw symbols representing a brain, partners, a puzzled face, or a dike with a hole in it.

6. After a few minutes, call time. Have the groups do a gallery walk, roaming the room to see one another's drawings. Facilitate discussion about the words and symbols that came to mind for the topic.

>> Invitation to Summarize

Summarization, the ability to capture the essence of a large piece of information in a small amount of words, is one of the most important thinking skills for enhancing learner achievement. Summarization that is shared also provides learners with the opportunity to review the content several times, enhancing retention. The Invitation to Summarize activity is a simple, creative way to add summarization to any presentation content.

How To

1. Obtain generic party invitations from a local store.

2. Complete the inside of the invitation with the following information:
   - What: Summarize your learning in five words or less
   - Place: Right here
   - Date and Time: Right now
   - RSVP: To the class

3. Change the "what" on each invitation so that they are slightly different. Include any of the following prompts:
   - Summarize your learning in ten words or less.
   - Summarize your learning in a rhyme.
   - Summarize your learning in a cheer
   - Summarize your learning in an acronym.

4. Place the invitations into the accompanying envelopes.

5. Ask participants to form groups of three to five people. Have someone from each group choose an invitation from your selection.

6. Provide the groups with three minutes to create their summary and be ready to share with the larger group.

7. Ask for a group to volunteer to go first, and then continue around the room.

>>> Learning Time Lines

Learners often experience great change throughout the course of a training. One way to capture this growth is through a Learning Time Line. This simple activity captures the communal experience in a colorful, visual way for all to see how far they have come!

How To

1. Obtain a roll of white craft paper that is 12 to 18 inches wide.

2. Hang long strips of the paper, horizontally, on the walls around the classroom.

3. Make sure that colored markers are available on tables.

4. At appropriate points during the workshop, ask two or three people to go to the Learning Time Line and document the last section of learning with simple graphics, words and phrases. Emphasize that stick figures are perfect; no one is expected to be a great artist!

5. Continue to add to the Time Line throughout the day.

6. If desired, draw attention to the Time Line before a break or near the end of the session to acknowledge all that has been accomplished throughout the day.

7. Take photos of some of the sections that capture the learning particularly well. These can make a great addition to a workplace blog or newsletter.

>> Personal Progress Bars

Academic researchers (Silver, Strong and Perini, 2007) tell us that successful lifelong learners are skilled at reflecting on their progress while they are learning, not just when the experience is finished. Rather than waiting for a test score or a grade to tell them how they are doing, successful students are adept at contemplating and analyzing their experience as they go along, making necessary adjustments to lead to success. Personal Progress Bars are tools to help participants reflect at several stages of a workshop, and can provide the facilitator with important information about his students.

How To

1. Provide participants with a Personal Progress Bar (at right) or ask them to draw a similar rectangle on a piece of paper. I like to have one bar for each of the learning objectives.

2. Ask everyone to silently reflect on each objective, and then shade the bar so that it represents their current level of knowledge and skill.

3. If desired, ask participants to share with a neighbor.

4. Midway through the workshop, ask participants to return to their progress bars and update them to show current levels. Suggest they use a different-colored writing utensil. Repeat this again just before the end of the session.

Personal Progress Bars (continued)

Shade in the *progress bars* to show your current levels.

0%	50%	100%

My knowledge and skills related to _____.

0%	50%	100%

My knowledge and skills related to _____.

0%	50%	100%

My knowledge and skills related to _____.

0%	50%	100%

My knowledge and skills related to _____.

0%	50%	100%

My knowledge and skills related to _____.

≫ Pass the Plate

Pass the Plate is a high-energy activity that encourages learners to generate a wide variety of ideas, and exposes all to creative thinking. It also has a hint of competition to boost adrenaline.

How To

1. Place participants in groups of three to five people, and provide each group with a plastic disposable plate and a water-based marker.

2. Explain that you will give them a word. One of the group members is to write the word in the center of the plate. For example, the word might be "trust."

3. Once the word has been written, tell the participants that they will have two minutes to generate as many synonyms for the word as possible. Each group member is to take a turn and write a synonym on the plate around the edge. The plate is to be passed around the group as quickly as possible. If someone cannot think of a word, she cannot pass, but someone else in the group can help her out.

4. Explain that each word will generate points, but the most points will be awarded to words that are not found on any other plate.

5. After the time period is finished, help participants determine the points for their group. Award 1000 points for each word on the plate, and 5000 points for any word that no other group has written.

6. When finished, simply rinse the plates off and store for another time.

>> Puzzle Piece Connections

One of the things that brain researchers are sure of is that new information being received by the brain must connect to previously stored information in order for it to move into long-term memory. The more connections that are made, the thicker the myelin sheath becomes, which strengthens the neural pathway making it more accessible for retrieval (Sprenger, 2005.) Puzzle Piece Connections provides a visual, tactile way to encourage learners to make connections.

How to

1. Make copies onto colored paper of the single jigsaw puzzle piece on the next page. Cut out and laminate each puzzle piece.

2. Obtain a jigsaw puzzle piece paper punch from a scrapbooking company and cut small jigsaw puzzle pieces.

3. Distribute small puzzle pieces to each table or group.

4. Ask everyone to reflect on their prior experiences and knowledge and make a connection to the new learning. Explain that once they have chosen a connection, they should write a word or phrase on their puzzle piece that represents the connection.

5. When everyone has finished writing, direct each group to build a puzzle by joining their pieces and sharing their connections.

6. When each small group has had sufficient time to share, hand each group one of the larger, laminated puzzle pieces and a dry erase marker. Ask them to summarize their discussion by writing one word or phrase on the larger piece.

7. Call on each group to come up to the board or wall and stick up its puzzle piece, explaining the word they captured. Continue until a larger puzzle has been put together that all can see.

continued—

Puzzle Piece Connections (continued)

≫ Sticky Dot Voting

Colored sticky dots are a versatile material that can be used in myriad ways. The "restickable" dots are even more versatile because participants can change their minds about where to place them. This is especially helpful when using them for a voting activity.

How To

1. Provide everyone with colored sticky dots. They should each be given the same amount so they will have an equal voice. Usually, two or three dots of different colors will suffice for most activities.

2. Project or print a legend to match and value the dots. For example, green dots = high priority, yellow dots = low priority.

3. Make a voting ballot on a piece of chart paper. For example, participants might vote on favorite ideas from a brainstormed list, important next actions or two different versions of a mission statement.

4. Direct each participant to bring up his or her sticky dots and stick them next to the items they value the most.

5. When everyone has voted, allow participants to view the votes and decide if they would like to move their dot(s) to another place.

6. Discuss with the group the outcome of the voting.

Variations

If participants have a paper handout, sticky dots can be used in many other ways. The visual and tactile nature of the dots makes them a simple way to increase engagement. For example, individuals can be encouraged to stick a dot next to:

- three questions from a lengthy list of questions
- five things they will add to their repertoire
- the one best idea from the morning session

>> Symbolic Summary

Nonlinguistic representations can be a strong memory enhancer for learners. The Symbolic Summary strategy encourages participants to augment their notes with quick, symbolic representations of their learning.

How To

1. Determine how many key concepts (four, six or eight) you want to reinforce with the use of the Symbolic Summary.

2. Provide everyone with a loose sheet of plain white paper and ask them to fold the paper into fourths, sixths, or eighths.

3. After the first concept has been taught, tell participants that they will have 45 seconds to draw a quick picture in the first space on their paper. The picture is to represent what they just learned, without using any words. Explain that the drawings should be simple, such as icons, logos, or symbols, rather than extremely detailed.

4. When 35 seconds have passed, give participants a ten-second countdown. Then ask everyone to turn and share their drawing with a neighbor. If desired, solicit one or two people to share with the group.

5. Continue with each key concept, filling the paper with symbolic drawings.

⟫ Text Message Summary

Text Messaging is a popular communication shortcut that can be used to practice succinct summarization of new learning.

How To

1. Copy the Text Message Cell Phone reproducible on the following page and distribute one to each participant.

2. Direct everyone to write a text message summary of their learning in the screen area, as if they were texting to a friend. Encourage them to use some of the shortcuts and alternative spelling that they might normally use when texting.

3. Encourage participants to share their summaries with the group. This can be done verbally, or the cell phones can be shown under a document camera.

Variations

- Use text messaging as an exit slip. Near the end of the class period, distribute the paper cell phones and direct participants to write a text message describing one thing they learned in class, or one thing they still have questions about.

- Use Internet sites such as www.polleverywhere.com to do live polling with your audience. Participants can use their cell phones to text in a response to a question the facilitator has designed in advance. The website is projected onto the screen and everyone can watch their text message responses being received in real time.

continued—

Text Message Summary (continued)

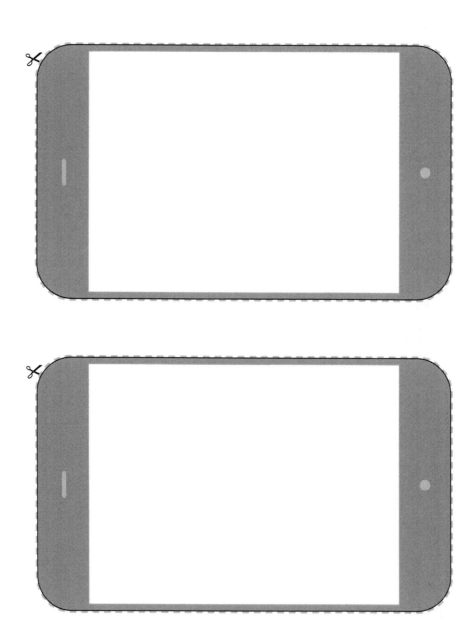

≫ Vote with Your Feet

Ongoing assessment is a necessary part of effective instruction. Vote with Your Feet utilizes a kinesthetic response to give facilitators some quick assessment information. It also provides participants with a chance to share opinions and connect more personally to the content.

How To

1. Make two signs—one that says Strongly Agree and another that says Strongly Disagree.

2. Post the Strongly Disagree sign on the far left side of the front wall of the classroom. Post the Strongly Agree sign on the far right side of the front wall.

3. Explain to participants that this represents a continuum, from strongly disagree to strongly agree, with many intermediate positions.

4. Ask everyone to stand. Explain that you will read a statement to them. They are to move and stand along the imaginary continuum based on their opinion of the statement.

5. Read your statement and then direct everyone to "Vote with their feet."

6. Lead a discussion by asking everyone to look around, make observations, draw conclusions, etc. Ask a few individuals standing in opposite places to explain why they chose their positions.

≫ Wikki Stix

One of the most versatile materials a facilitator can have on hand is a set of Wikki Stix. Wikki Stix are colorful strings covered in wax. They can be used to form all kinds of shapes, even more easily than pipe cleaners. With adults, they are best used to develop symbolic representations of a new concept.

How To

1. Provide each small group with 10 to 15 Wikki Stix (available from www.wikkistix.com). Wikki Stix store well in zipped plastic baggies.

2. When introducing Wikki Stix to your audience, allow them to experiment with them for a few minutes.

3. Direct participants to use their Wikki Stix to build a symbolic representation of their learning.

4. After a few minutes, ask everyone to stand. Move from table to table to see the Wikki Stix creations and hear the explanations.

5. Take a photo of each creation, perhaps to share on a company website, as part of a celebration slide show or to e-mail six weeks later as a reminder of the learning.

⫸ Word Toss

Comprehension and retention of new terms may be an essential underlying component of your workshop. If so, do what the vocabulary experts recommend: have learners practice the vocabulary in a variety of ways. Word Toss engages learners through auditory, visual and tactile means, while adding a game-like quality to the task.

How To

1. Place participants into pairs and provide each pair with a die.

2. Project the Word Toss sheet onto your screen or make copies and distribute to pairs.

3. Explain *non-example* to the group through modeling. A non-example is something that is not an antonym of the word, may be close in meaning, but is not a synonym of the word. If the focus word is *allege* a non-example might be *hint*.

4. Choose the word or phrase that needs more in-depth exploration. Direct participants to roll the dice and do whatever the number indicates.

5. After about 15 seconds, direct them to roll again.

6. Facilitate sharing either by small groups or whole groups.

continued—

Non-Example

Sentence

Synonym

Antonym

Description

Draw It

References

Cain, S. 2012. *Quiet: The Power of Introverts in a World that Can't Stop Talking*. NY: Crown.

Clance, P.R. and Imes, S. A.1978. "The Imposter Phenomenon in High Achieving Women." *Psycotherapy: Theory, Research and Practice* 15, 241–247.

Clark, K. 1998. *Life is Change, Growth is Optional*. St.Paul: Center for Executive Planning.

Dale, E. 1946. *Audio-Visual Methods in Teaching*. NY: Dryden Press.

Darling-Hammond, L. and Richardson, N. 2009. "Teaching Learning: What Matters?" *Educational Leadership* 66(5): 62–69.

Gladwell, M. 2000. *The Tipping Point: How Little Things Can Make a Big Difference*. NY: Back Bay Books.

Gladwell, M. 2008. *Outliers: The Story of Success*. NY: Little, Brown.

Guskey, T. R. 2000. *Evaluating Professional Development*. Thousand Oaks, CA: Corwin Press.

Guskey, T.R. 2014. "Planning Professional Learning." *Educational Leadership* 71(8): 11–16.

Knowles, M. 1970. *The Modern Practice of Adult Education: Andragogy Versus Pedagogy*. Chicago: Association Press

Marzano, R., Pickering, D. and Pollock, J. 2001. *Classroom Instruction that Works*. Alexandria, VA: Association for Supervision and Curriculum Development.

NASA (National Aeronautics and Space Administration). 2003. "Report of Columbia Accident Investigation Board, Volume 1." National Aeronautics and Space Administration. Last updated March 5, 2006.

Pink, D. 2012. *To Sell Is Human: The Surprising Truth About Moving Others*. NY: Penguin [iBook].

Prensky, M. 2012. *Brain Gain: Technology and the Quest for Digital Wisdom*. NY: Palgrave MacMillan.

Reeves, D. 2010. *Transforming Professional Development into Student Results*. Alexandria, VA: ASCD.

Reynolds, G. 2008. *Presentation Zen*. Berkeley, CA: New Riders.

Roam, D. 2008. *The Back of the Napkin*. NY: Penguin.

Silver, H., Strong, R. and Perini, M. 2007. *The Strategic Teacher*. Alexandria, VA: ASCD.

Sprenger, M. 2005. *How to Teach so Students Remember*. Alexandria, VA: ASCD.

Sprenger, M. 2010. *Brain-based Teaching in the Digital Age*. Alexandria, VA: ASCD.

Willis, J. 2007. *Brain-Friendly Strategies for the Inclusion Classroom*. Alexandria, VA: ASCD.

Made in the USA
Lexington, KY
07 August 2019